CW00504672

For anyone who might be daunted by
Muslims about Jesus Christ, here is
a whole series of questions for con'
in a simple set of topics. It is full of
explanations, presented simply and briefly, and does not demand
any expert knowledge of Islam. As someone who has engaged in
this kind of evangelism, I can see that it could be a really useful
resource, and I warmly commend it.

Graham Nicholls, *Director of Affinity*

This is a very significant work which every Christian can benefit
from reading, and particularly Christians interacting with Muslim
friends. I note that the authors speak of and with the Muslims
as friends and so win their respect. Muslims like questions and
are normally happy to discuss their faith and Christianity. But
what to ask them? This book contains a wide spectrum of basic
questions that won't be offensive, but will be challenging. And
gives answers! The book follows our Lord's approach to people of
His day: He asked them questions and answered theirs!

Dr John Peet, *former missionary elder, Grace Church Guildford*

In the clash between the two antagonistic world views, Islam and
Christianity, Beth and Tim help us to grasp both intelligently. At
the same time, they suggest helpful dialogues with Muslims. In
the process of reading this book, one will solidify one's Biblical
knowledge and faith in Christ.

Silas Tostes, *Brazilian Evangelical Alliance*
Managing Council President

Questions to Ask Your Muslim Friends is a great resource to help
Christians get past that initial fear of opening up a conversation.
If we truly love our Muslim friends, we must take the initiative to
bring them the good news. This timely resource will help you do
just that!

Dr. James R. White, *Apologist, theologian, author, and director*
of Alpha and Omega Ministries, Phoenix, Arizona

Beth and Tim share a passion for Christians to confidently engage their Muslim friends in conversations about faith. We need Christians to be bold and confident in sharing the Gospel. Sometimes Christians feel that they don't really know where to start when discussing their respective faiths with Muslims. This is why the authors have written this book. It is not just a beginner's guide, though. There is some rich content to engage with and discuss with your friends. If you would like to challenge and encourage your Muslim friends to follow Jesus, this book will equip you, encourage you, and embolden you to be an effective witness. I hope that many people read it and make use of it. I pray that God will use it to bring many Muslims to true faith in Jesus. For those who are weary of the complexities of such conversations that might arise as they engage with Muslim friends, remember that, 'Within the complexities and complications of conversations, there can be conversions!'

Pastor Ade Omooba MBE, *Co-founder, Christian Concern*

Questions to Ask Your Muslim Friends gets right to the heart of how to have meaningful conversations with Muslim friends and acquaintances that clearly lead them to faith in the Lord Jesus Christ! Drawing on years of ministry and extensive experience encountering Islam and its claims, the authors raise penetrating questions that open up opportunities to effectively share the life-giving truths of the Gospel and answer important questions that one might be reluctant to ask. This small book is a valuable resource for anyone who lovingly wants to help Muslims come to saving faith in Christ.

Stephen Krstulovich, Ph.D., *Director of Research* and
Donna Hardee Krstulovich, Ph.D., *International Trainer,*
Global Initiative: Reaching Muslim Peoples

This is a timely book in several respects. This is because we live in a unique era of history wherein the persistent historic Islamic opposition to conversion of Muslims to Christianity is no longer airtight! The availability of knowledge about the Bible is widespread through the media and mission work, thus opening the door for Muslim seekers to discover on their own or with the help of Christian believers, the true Biblical message and belief system. As a result, we discover that in almost any country in the world, Muslim or otherwise, there are converts to Christianity from Islam, and in many cases, large communities of converts out of Islam to Christianity.

This development poses challenges to those who had been raised in a Christian society and have accepted Christ as their Lord and Saviour. All of a sudden, they are faced with the challenge to explain doctrinal issues, as well as social and political issues — since Islam, being an all-encompassing 'system', demands answers in all spheres of life.

The main advantage of this book by Peltola and Dieppe is that it challenges the serious Christian and Muslim to treat the issues with utmost objectivity. Through carefully constructed questions and answers, the Christian and the Muslim will be able to identify the underlying factors which would lead one to 'believe.' As a result, the reader receives first-hand answers and is guided to get deeper into the issues by examining the suggested resources or by carrying out of further inquiry.

I must congratulate the authors for hitting a balance and providing for a mechanism that allows any seeker, Christian or Muslim, to dig deeper into one's own faith and relationship to those on the opposite side.

Atif Debs, *Co-Author with Sam Solomon: 'Not the Same God—*
Is the Qur'anic Allah the LORD God of the Bible?'

This book is dynamite, jam-packed with powerful questions to trigger meaningful spiritual encounters. When talking with your Muslim friends, don't be caught on the back foot. This is a must-have tool for anyone who has a heart to share the love of Jesus with Muslims. It not only suggests great questions but it also puts tools in your hands so you can set the agenda for a life-changing conversation.

Dr Mark Durie, *Director, Institute for Spiritual Awareness*

An incredibly helpful resource for any Christian wanting to know how to have meaningful conversations with Muslims about Jesus Christ.

Beth and Tim have given us a vast gold mine of insightful and searching questions that will help us open up productive conversations with our Muslim friends and point them towards Jesus.

Do you desire to show Muslims the truth and beauty of Jesus but struggle to know how to open up a conversation? Do you ever want to challenge your Muslim friends about their beliefs but fear offending them in the process? Learning from the example of Jesus, Beth and Tim offer us a profound, liberating and yet simple method: asking questions! This book is packed full of brilliant questions that we can make use of. A superb resource that you will go back to again and again.

There is an old proverb that says that it is harder to ask a good question than it is to give a good answer. Beth and Tim have given us a rich treasure trove of questions that we can use to open up meaningful conversations with our Muslim friends and neighbours and point them towards Jesus.

Michael Ots, *Evangelist*

With Islam as the second largest religion in the world today, there is an urgent need for Christians to be equipped to confidently witness to their Muslim friends. This superb book meets that need in an accessible and yet uncompromising manner. The authors suggest questions which can be used to open up discussion and provoke dialogue with the aim of leading Muslims to faith in Christ. Readers will benefit from the deep understanding displayed by the authors of how Islamic teaching contrasts with Biblical teaching. I wholeheartedly recommend this book as an excellent resource for all those who want to see their Muslim friends impacted by the life-giving power of the Gospel.

Archbishop Professor Thomas Schirrmacher, PhD, DD,
Secretary General of the World Evangelical Alliance

With this book, Beth and Tim have successfully given us a unique and outstanding tool for evangelizing our Muslim friends whilst deepening our understanding of Islam. With a fresh and readable style they skilfully employ a conversational, Socratic method to both engage the reader and teach an evangelistic methodology. The traditional rabbinic technique of using questions to engage with other questions was employed by the Lord Jesus himself – an approach which presses our conversation partners to think and engage critically. Wearing its profound depth of scholarship lightly, this is a substantial work that will not just add weight to your shelves, but also to your arguments and witness.

Rev. Dr. Joseph Boot,
Founder and President of the Ezra Institute

After his encounter with the Samaritan woman, as recorded in John's Gospel, Jesus says to his disciples, "I sent you to reap what you have not worked for. Others have done the hard work..." (John 4:38).

Beth Peltola and Tim Dieppe have done a fantastic service to the church with this brief but profoundly detailed aid to conversation with Muslim friends.

Christians often find themselves on the back foot when talking to Muslims, struggling to answer questions about the divinity of Christ, the Trinity and charges about the Bible having been corrupted.

This book takes a different approach, one modelled on Jesus' own methodology, by giving dozens of penetrating questions to ask Muslims, which will encourage them to think, and sow seeds of doubt in their minds about the reliability of the Qur'an and the Prophet Muhammad.

Many former Muslims will testify that beginning to doubt Islam was the first step on their journey to knowing Christ.

In ten tightly written chapters, supplemented with seven pages of resources and fourteen pages of referenced footnotes, Beth and Tim have neatly summarised scholarship spanning centuries, from the very best Christian apologists. The result will give confidence to young Christians with little experience of engaging Muslims, and refine the skills of experienced evangelists.

At a time in history when more Muslims are coming to Christ than ever before and when the moral, historical and ethical foundations of Islam are crumbling, this is a superb resource to have at hand and should be read and re-read by anyone serious about introducing their Muslims friends to the real Lord and Saviour.

I highly recommend it.

Dr Peter Saunders, *Chief Executive,*
International Christian Medical and Dental Association (ICMDA)

What a wonderful book! Full of powerful, accessible resources to equip all of us to share Jesus with our Muslim friends and neighbours. Glory!!

Over the past 30 years I have read countless books and articles about this kind of mission. Over and over again, the writers assume that Islam and Christianity share some or most of the core foundations. However, one of the first lessons we learned was that Allah is not at all like Jesus or the Trinity as a whole. We used to think that it was respectful to talk to our Muslim friends as if we were speaking about the same god, but as we discovered, that led to much unnecessary conflict. Their god just does not have eternal Father/Son relationships – and they seem to find it offensive to even think of their god in that way. Their god cannot possibly become a human being, suffer, or die ... and rise again – the very thought of that is blasphemous to them. We need to be bold, confident and passionate if we are to communicate the glory and wonder of Jesus to the followers of Muhammad.

This book from Beth and Tim is so helpful because it not only helps Christians to become more deeply rooted in the genuine ancient faith of Church, but it also trains us to engage with our Muslim friends in fruitful, serious and meaningful ways. I cannot wait to use these questions in my own conversations!

It is so good to ask our Muslim friends, "What do you think Christians believe?" because that opens up great conversations that can clear away myths and fables. Comparing Jesus and Muhammad is very powerful: childhoods, lifestyles, miracles, sin, violence, slavery, prophecy etc. Again, opening up genuine questions about the content, clarity and conception of the Quran is a powerful tool, especially when the entire self-confidence of Islam rests on claims about that book. Especially valuable is the way Chapter 6 lists out the things that Islam says about women.

Whether we are dealing with violence, historical inaccuracies, misunderstandings about Christianity or the challenging questions that Muslims ask Christians, this book is the best single resource for Christians who want to share Jesus with their Muslim friends, colleagues, family and neighbours. Praise God!

Rev Dr Paul Blackham, *church planter and author of the 'Book by Book' Bible study guides*

QUESTIONS TO ASK YOUR MUSLIM FRIENDS
A Closer Look at Islamic Beliefs and Texts

QUESTIONS TO ASK YOUR MUSLIM FRIENDS
A Closer Look at Islamic Beliefs and Texts

Beth Peltola

and

Tim Dieppe

Wilberforce Publications
London

Published in Great Britain in 2022 by
Wilberforce Publications Limited
70 Wimpole Street, London W1G 8AX

ISBN 978-1-9995842-8-3

Printed by Amazon

Contents

Dedication

Beth and Tim would like to dedicate this book to their Muslim friends, with whom they hope to continue to have many fruitful and enlightening conversations.

We pray that you will come to a sure and certain knowledge of the salvation, for which our Lord Jesus Christ suffered and died.

We can testify that trusting in Jesus as God, Saviour and friend, is better than life itself and worth any and every sacrifice you might have to make.

He died so that we may become righteous like Him, and have life everlasting (New Testament – 2 Corinthians, Chapter 5).

Foreword

I am delighted to write this foreword, having known the authors, Beth, as my student in Qur'anic studies, and Tim, as a colleague at Christian Concern.

To their credit, this work contrasts greatly in relation to many other books on outreach to Muslims, especially in that most of those books take positions of using the so-called "similarities" between the Qur'an and the Bible to build "bridges of understanding". Such approaches, which depend on illustrations from the Qur'an to try to show agreement with the Bible, miss the central theological position of Islam, which is anti-Bible and anti-Christ. These hyper-contextualisation approaches have gone much too far and some have morphed into the so-called 'Insider Movements' which can compromise the distinctiveness of the Gospel. Thankfully, the authors of this book have started from the sound basis that these similarities are only superficial, whereas the fundamental differences are glaringly obvious. This wise stance allows them to speak of Christ truthfully, without resorting to unhelpful theological bridge-building.

Beth and Tim explain that this is a book primarily for Christians to prepare them for engaging in substantive conversations with Muslims who may or may not be literate in the tenets of Islam. Therefore, they propose a method based on the posing of questions to open the door for theological interactions. The authors are of the opinion that this is nothing more than the application of the 'Jesus method' of answering questions by posing other questions. In the process, the reader is encouraged to generate his or her own questions and to come up with responses and explanations like the ones given by the authors.

They suggest that by posing questions, the interested Christian reader can come to an understanding of the Islamic mindset in the light of the relevant Biblical positions which will answer the questions. Also, where the Muslims being addressed are more knowledgeable in their beliefs, the authors are able to suggest more difficult questions and to challenge the Muslim to come up with a satisfactory answer. The questions raised and answers given in the book are meant to provide only a starting point from which one may elaborate and think of other questions. On the other hand, the occasional Muslim reader may find it intriguing, and, depending on his or her spiritual journey, it might provoke a variety of reactions!

In short, *Questions to Ask Your Muslim Friends – A Closer Look at Islamic Beliefs and Texts* attempts to achieve two goals: (a) to improve the Biblical knowledge of the missionary for Christ; and (b) to equip him or her with a basic understanding of Islam's doctrines and practices. This approach sits at the boundary of direct discussion of the relevant theological issues and a missiological methodology for reaching Muslims to Christ.

From my perspective, I have always advocated a full separation between understanding the theological issues, and the methodologies for reaching Muslims. Theology must drive missiology and not the other way around. Unfortunately, many missionaries have taken short cuts, prioritised missiological methods, and ended up compromising the theological message. The authors here have attempted to bridge these two considerations with their question-and-answer approach.

Thus, Beth and Tim have produced a thought-provoking book which can be used as a learning tool and reference document. Thankfully, the substantial endnotes and selected resource documents provide ample materials for the serious reader to become more informed, and thus more effective, on these critical issues.

Sam Solomon, former Islamic Jurist and
author of *Not the Same God: Is the Qur'anic Allah
the Lord God of the Bible?*
(Wilberforce Publications, 2016)

March 2022

Acknowledgements

We are very grateful to those who have read through our manuscript as theologians, historians and grammarians!

A big thank you to Sam Solomon for his generous foreword and his invaluable teaching and input and brave stance on Islam over many years. A shout-out to Rev Andrew Stewart, who looked over our theological and conversational points. Dr Mark Durie provided some helpful feedback, and ideas for future books! Dr. Paul Blackham's material was inspirational in helping to communicate Christ through all the Scriptures, especially in relation to speaking about God with Muslim friends. We would also like to thank Dr Jay Smith for his inspiration and input and example in debating and witnessing to Muslims at Speakers' Corner for many years. Jay kindly read through the manuscript and suggested some helpful edits. Any errors remain entirely the authors'.

Many people have encouraged us to write this book and make the material available to a wider audience. Our thanks to the team at Wilberforce Publications for making that happen, editing various versions of the manuscript and bringing it to production. Given the numerous references and theological and historical details, we know this was a big task to take on, and we are most grateful to you.

As authors, we enjoyed working on this together. It takes time, patience and discussion, together with well-needed healthy debate, to bring together two minds from different church backgrounds and experiences, to complete a detailed book such as this. We are thankful for the opportunity to write this book and look forward to seeing how the Lord will use the material in the lives of those who read it.

Most of all we are grateful to our Heavenly Father who, compelled by His love for us, sent his Son, the Lord Jesus, to die in our place. We stand in awe and worship the Lord Jesus – that though He could have called down the angels from heaven to take Him off that cross, stayed on it for our sakes. We delight in the

Holy Spirit who guides our thoughts and aids our understanding of the height, depth and width of God's love and engagement with us, and empowers hearty conversations with God too!

Introduction

Imagine feeling confident to effectively share your faith with Muslim friends. Maybe you already do, maybe you don't. Either way, the aim of this book is to empower Christians to witness effectively when engaging Muslim friends in conversations about faith.

Many Christians feel that they do not know where to start in discussing their faith with Muslims. This book provides ideas for starting a conversation, with several suggestions for questions to ask. Even if you are experienced in discussing Gospel issues with those who do not agree with you, we hope you will find this book a thought-provoking and helpful addition to your experience.

We do this because we love Muslims, but we also love truth. The Bible calls us to refute ideologies such as Islam, but we are also called to love all people – including Muslims. The aim is not to criticise Muslims but rather, to challenge and stimulate our Muslim friends to think critically about their religion. As Christians, we will want to talk about the Gospel because it is important to us, and because we care about our Muslim friends' salvation, which cannot be found in Islam.

In a respectful manner, questions like the ones suggested here can be asked in your own words. If you are asking Muslim friends to consider their beliefs critically, you need to be prepared to engage in discussions with them over a period of time. You may also need to research the answers to these questions, or other questions that they may ask, in more depth than is presented here. Some suggested resources for further study are given throughout, and at the end of the book.

That said, part of the aim here is to show that you do not need to be an expert to discuss your faith with Muslims. Confidence in the lifechanging power of the Gospel (Romans 1:16) is the only requirement.

1

Why Ask Questions?

Do you realise that Jesus is recorded as asking over two hundred questions in the Gospels?[1] He frequently responded to a question with another question. His questions often got to the heart of the matter and were powerful and effective teaching tools. Here are some examples:

"Who do you say that I am?" (Matthew 16:15)

"Why do you call Me good?" (Matthew 19:17)

"The baptism of John – where was it from? From heaven or from men?" (Matthew 21:25)

"What do you think about the Christ? Whose Son is He?" (Matthew 22:42)

"How can you escape the condemnation of hell?" (Matthew 23:33) "Why do you reason about these things in your hearts?" (Mark 2:8)

"Do you not perceive that whatever enters a man from outside cannot defile him …?" (Mark 7:18)

"What was it you disputed among yourselves on the road?" (Mark 9:33)

"Which of you by worrying can add one cubit to his stature?" (Luke 12:25)

"Does this offend you?" (John 6:61)

"Do you believe this?" (John 11:26)

"Do you love Me?" (John 21:17)

These questions do not always have a simple answer. They force people to think. This was Jesus' intention. It is also the intention of this book. Our suggested questions are designed to prompt your Muslim friends to think about their faith – perhaps in ways they have not done before. They are intended to get to the heart of what your friends believe, and why. They are also intended to demonstrate the many differences between Islam and Christianity, and to help your friends realise that the 'truth claims' of Islam are false.

The importance of asking questions

Many Muslims are fearful of questioning their beliefs and practices, due to Qur'anic commands to obey Allah and his messenger (Muhammad), in the hope that they may attain a place in paradise after death. In the Islamic view of god, Allah is a master – not a Heavenly Father who has made it possible for people to approach Him as sons and daughters, asking questions, and responding in close relationship. Questioning is discouraged in the Qur'an.

"Obey Allah and obey the Messenger." (Q 5:92 Yusuf Ali)[2]

"O ye who believe! Ask not questions about things which, if made plain to you, may cause you trouble. But if ye ask about things when the Qur'an is being revealed, they will be made plain to you, Allah will forgive those: for Allah is Oft-forgiving, Most Forbearing. Some people before you did ask such questions, and on that account lost their faith." (Q 5:101-102 Yusuf Ali)

The need for boldness

Muslims often enjoy robust discussions or debates about these issues because this type of engagement tends to conform with Islamic cultures. The majority of Muslims respect Christians who can confidently defend their faith and challenge Islam, because this fits their view of a religious person. Often, they have never met a Christian who is able and willing to talk openly about faith issues. Christians need to be bold in talking about their faith with Muslims. We must be bold because it is Biblical. The apostles prayed for great boldness to speak about Jesus (Acts 4:29). We also must pray for boldness; to be bold is culturally appropriate for traditional Muslims. Most Muslims see faith as a public issue, and therefore expect people to be open in public about their faith. Any reluctance to speak out about your faith is likely to be viewed as weakness by your Muslim friends. This means that we need to be particularly bold in talking about faith with Muslims – beyond what is normal in Western culture. For example, if you believe that Muhammad was not a prophet, you should clearly say so. Muslims will expect you to say what you believe, and any reluctance to do so may be seen as a sign of weakness, to say nothing of appearing dishonest. However, for those living in countries ruled by Islamic law, caution and wisdom are needed, as such a statement can lead to the death sentence.

This book is intended to help and encourage Christians to question Muslims confidently about their faith so that they too can come to experience, know, and walk with the Living Lord Jesus Christ. Several of the questions in this book require no background knowledge but can be very effective avenues for sharing your faith. Ask the questions that you feel comfortable with, using your own style of conversation. They are but suggested questions. Feel free to amend them as you see fit. It is important not to shy away from talking about your faith with Muslims – and never to compromise the Gospel.

'But my Muslim friend is liberal'

You may be thinking of a Muslim friend who is a modern, second or third generation 'Western Muslim'. They may have shared with you an attractive, rosy picture of Islam and Muhammad. Perhaps you have been told that Islam means 'peace', and that Muhammad was a man of peace.[3] What many Christians fail to understand is the vast gulf between the ideals of a moderate Muslim and what their actual texts teach.

Muslims are generally supposed to read the Qur'an in Arabic only; the same applies to set prayers. However, many Muslims do not understand Arabic. It is widely thought that only about 20%[4] of Muslims globally are Arabic speakers. Whatever the exact percentage, many Muslims have never read the Qur'an from cover to cover in their own language, let alone in Arabic. This means that most Muslims are uninformed about what their holy book – or the biography of Muhammad, or the Islamic traditions – essentially teach. It is also worth being aware that some modern English translations (and translations in other languages) do not accurately reflect what is in the Arabic text of the Qur'an. This is especially true of versions of the Qur'an given out in Islamic mission settings.

This book has been written by Christian researchers who have studied the Islamic texts, read differing Islamic theological positions, and spent hours discussing faith issues with Muslim friends, as well as debating with Muslims, including Muslim missionaries to Britain. It is a book based on the texts of Islam using what is known as 'the book and the man' approach.[5]

'The book and the man'

A religion, if true to its source, should be judged by its holy text, and by its founder. For Islam, that is the Qur'an (their book) and the life of Muhammad (their man). For Christianity, that is the Bible (our book) and the life of Jesus (our man). In conversations you have with a Muslim, at some point it will come back to these two – 'the book and the man'. It is helpful to bear in mind when you enter into discussions with Muslims, so that you don't get side-tracked.[6]

Is it right to try to 'win' arguments?

You may have heard the oft-quoted phrase: 'Win an argument, lose the person.' We want to re-word this to be more in keeping with the Biblical mandate and the example of the early Church. What if the Church were to 'win the argument *and* win the person'? We are not talking about scoring points or forcing your views. The Bible presents reasoned arguments about God, life, creation and salvation. We should not therefore shy away from reasoning about these things with our Muslim friends. The questions in this book are tools for you to use, through which the Holy Spirit can work His transforming power in the lives of those with whom you communicate. The Bible exhorts us to set forth the truth plainly (2 Corinthians 4:2), demolish arguments against the Biblical God (2 Corinthians 10:5), and *always be ready to give a defence to everyone who asks you to give the reason for the hope that is in you* (1 Peter 3:15). The Bible provides many examples of God's people – the prophets and believers of old – engaging in discussion and debate, and presenting clear arguments for truth.

A quick perusal of the book of Acts throws up words such as 'confounded ... [by] proving' (Acts 9:22), 'vigorously refuted' (Acts 18:28), 'spoke boldly', 'reasoning', and 'persuading'

(Acts 19:8). This does not always mean that the message is accepted, but it does mean that the case for the truth has been well presented. Biblical boldness enables us to contend in the power of God – loving Muslims while critiquing Islam.

Using the Old Testament to share about the Lord Jesus

You will notice, as you go through this book, that we love to share the Gospel from the books of Moses. Christians know that the Bible's message has never changed:[7] Jesus is the same yesterday, today and forever (Hebrews 13:8). This means that the divine Son has never changed; He didn't suddenly come into existence just two thousand years ago. The Bible tells us that Jesus created us (Genesis 1:1-3; 26-27; John 1:1-14; Hebrews 1:2) and is the seen face of the invisible God:

He is the image of the invisible God, the firstborn over all creation. For by Him all things were created that are in heaven and that are on earth, visible and invisible, whether thrones or dominions or principalities or powers. All things were created through Him and for Him. And He is before all things, and in him all things consist (Colossians 1:15-17).

If this is so, then the One from heaven – the seen LORD to whom prophets and people bowed down (Exodus 34:8; Judges 13:20-22), spoke with (Exodus 3) and ate a meal with (Genesis 18) throughout the Old Testament – cannot be the unseen Father but must be the seen Son. Anyone familiar with Old Testament passages will see Scripture after Scripture referring to God's people meeting with this LORD:[8] Adam and Eve (Genesis 3), Abraham and Sarah (Genesis 18), Hagar (Genesis 16), Moses (Exodus 3, 33), Joshua (Joshua 5), Aaron and Miriam (Numbers 12), Samson's mother (Judges 13), Samuel (1 Samuel 3:10, 21), David (Psalm 16:8; see also Acts 2:25-28), and many more throughout the Scriptures.[9]

If you have ever shared your faith with a Muslim friend, you would have realised that Muslims revere Moses and certain other Biblical prophets, yet it is important to know that the stories surrounding Islamic versions of our prophets are not the same, and always leave out the most important point of the Biblical stories – those moments when the priests, prophets, kings and ordinary people met the living, seen, named Lord! This statement might give you pause for thought, and it certainly will achieve a response from Muslim friends. There are multiple reasons for these omissions in Islamic texts, but they stem largely from Islamic teaching about Jesus. Here are some examples:

- Islam teaches that Jesus was created some two thousand years ago.
- Islam teaches that God is not a man, so Jesus cannot be God.
- Islam teaches that Jesus' divinity was made up three hundred years after Jesus was born.
- Islam teaches that Jesus did not claim to be divine.

Muslims and Christians have two completely different starting points when it comes to understanding who God is. If Islam says god is unknowable and in a sense undefined, referred to just as 'the god' – a being that will never live with people (even in paradise), a god who never takes on human form because it is seen as beneath that god to do so, then it is easy to understand why Muslims have such an aversion to Jesus being God.

All of this stems from a contradictory view of God between Christianity and Islam. In Islam, god does not have a personal name – god is referred to as Allah, 'the god'. Some Muslims will object to using personal pronouns in reference to god, and prefer to simply state 'Allah'. Christians, however, speak about, and to, God as a friend, fully aware that our Saviour, Jesus, is a man: the man from heaven (1 Corinthians 15:47-49). A helpful distinction to make when speaking with Muslims, because it sets the Biblical God apart from the Islamic. This is the Christian way of thinking, stemming from Biblical teaching that all human beings are beautifully designed (Psalm 139:14) and made in God's image (Genesis 1:27-28).

The Bible is clear that God has always related to human beings personally, often in human form (Genesis 3:8-9; Exodus 3:2-6, 15:3, 33:11; Numbers 12:8; Philippians 2:5-11).[10] The Lord comes down to rescue (Exodus 3:2-10, 14:19, 24; Judges

6:11-23; Joshua 5:13-15; Jude 5), to serve (Isaiah 53; Matthew 26:14-39; John 13:1-16; Mark 10:45), and to die for all people (Leviticus 17:11; Matthew 26:14-39; John 3:16-17; Acts 20:28). He has communicated directly with human beings from the very beginning (Genesis 3:8-24), through history, and He will continue to do so into eternity (Revelation 21:3-6, 22:4).

It is truly thrilling to introduce the Scriptures to those who have not read them, to help them discover Jesus throughout the pages of the whole Bible.

Then she called the name of the LORD who spoke to her, You-Are-the-God-Who-Sees; for she said, "Have I also here seen Him who sees me?" (Genesis 16:13).

The Angel of the LORD appeared to him in a flame of fire from the midst of a bush... God called to him from the midst of the bush and said, "Moses, Moses!" And he said, "Here I am." Then He said, "Do not draw near this place. Take your sandals off your feet, for the place where you stand is holy ground." Moreover He said, "I am the God of your father — the God of Abraham, the God of Isaac, and the God of Jacob." And Moses hid his face, for he was afraid to look upon God (Exodus 3:2-6).

The LORD looked down upon the army of the Egyptians through the pillar of fire and cloud (Exodus 14:24).

Now the LORD descended in the cloud and stood with him [Moses] there, and proclaimed the name of the LORD. And the LORD passed before him and proclaimed, "The LORD, the LORD God, merciful and gracious, longsuffering, and abounding in goodness and truth" (Exodus 34:5-6).

... For today the LORD will appear to you (Leviticus 9:4).

Then the LORD came down in the cloud, and spoke to him, ... (Numbers 11:25).

Now the LORD came and stood and called as at other times, "Samuel, Samuel!" And Samuel answered, "Speak, for Your servant hears" (1 Samuel 3:10).

I saw the LORD standing by the altar (Amos 9:1).

This is a brief selection of verses from different time periods of history showing the LORD engaging with human beings – at times to rescue, at times to judge, and often to protect – with the end goal always being to bring humanity back to Himself, away from our own self-destructive tendencies and selfishness.

Pointing to Jesus through *all* of Scripture, in both the Old and New Testaments, helps to correct Islam's misinformed beliefs about Biblical history, such as:

- The New Testament has been corrupted and reports an incorrect version of Jesus.
- The New Testament was written too late to be accurate.
- The Gnostic or Nag Hammadi Gospels[11] have the correct renditions of Jesus.

These sorts of assertions stem from the belief that Jesus is only mentioned in the New Testament, and that true versions of His life were found only in late Gnostic writings. There are many good books responding to this critique, however. Perhaps the best responses come from the early Church Fathers who wrote against Gnostic ideas being developed from the middle of the 2nd century AD. These Church Fathers responded with the same trust in Jesus as the Apostles of Jesus – that Jesus is the Lord God, King of Kings, who died on a cross for our sins, rose again and now reigns on high, who will come back to destroy evil and establish peace and justice, to bring his church, described as His Bride, into His glorious eternal city to live with Him forever (Revelation 19-22). Now that is quite a sentence, but it has always been the position of the Church – from Genesis through to Revelation.[12]

Here are more misconceptions many of our Muslim friends will have about the Bible:

- The New Testament has a different view of God from the Old Testament.
- The Old Testament doesn't teach salvation through Jesus.
- Moses and the prophets did not know Jesus.

These are questions that many sceptics ponder, yet are easy to respond to. The best way to start is by doing a Bible study looking at the New Testament view of the Old Testament. The New Testament is integrally dependent on the Old, and many of its statements originate in some form in the Old Testament.

We go into more detail on some of the questions raised here, in the section: Questions Muslims Ask (pp 109ff).

To Muslims who may read this book

Contained within this book are some of the many questions Christians have about Islam. When a Christian reads the Bible and then the Qur'an, the vast differences between the two often lead the Christian to question why Islam seeks to undermine the most important elements of the Biblical message.

The Lord Jesus has told us: "the truth shall make you free" (John 8:32). Jesus also shows us the importance of questioning, discussing and challenging claims made about Him that differ from how He has revealed Himself from the beginning of history. By contrast, the Qur'an has replaced the real Jesus of history and the Bible with a surrogate, 'Isa', a Qur'anic prophet who stands in opposition to essential doctrines about the true Lord Jesus.

This book is written primarily for Christians, but if you are not a Christian reading it, we hope that it will also present clearly to you the Biblical view of God, seen in Jesus (Colossians 1:15) through both the Old and New Testaments. We also hope that you will engage in conversation with Christians in order to understand the vast differences between our beliefs, and why Christians believe that Jesus is the only Saviour of mankind.

Within these pages are many Biblical and Islamic references to help the reader discover the truth of the matter for themselves. Jesus states that He is the Way, the Truth, and the Life, and that no one comes to the Father except through Him (John 14:6). We also read that He is 'the Alpha and the Omega – the Beginning and the End...' (Revelation 21:6), the 'Prince of life' (Acts 3:15), and the leader of the armies of heaven (Revelation 19:11-16) who fights the evil that harms humanity and God's creation. If we accept a false view of Jesus, it is a grievous evil against God, because we are rejecting who God is. Bring it down to your own level: would you like to be rejected? No one would. Yet how much more serious it is when our eternal destiny depends on the Living Lord Jesus – our relationship with Him, trusting Him, and learning from Him about who He is and what He has done for us.

This is why Christians wish to engage with others on these matters. We encourage you to learn about what Christians believe, and truly search for the truth, for the truth will set you free (John 8:32) and open the way to eternal life (John 14:6).

2

Questions about Faith

The following questions require little or no knowledge of Islamic theology, but can open up profound issues of truth and lead to deep and meaningful conversations. Muslims will tend to have their own answers to these questions and will generally be comfortable talking about their beliefs. Let's dive in and start asking some questions about Islam and Muslims!

'How did you become a Muslim?'

This question is intended to highlight a key difference between Christianity and Islam. Most Muslims will say that they were born Muslim, or born in a Muslim country, or into a Muslim family. Converts to Islam will often make claims about the 'logic' of Islam, the simple 'oneness of Allah' compared with the 'Trinity', the perception of a 'perfect Qur'an', the 'ennoblement of women', the 'clear rules', the 'moral standards' versus the immorality of the 'Christian West'. Among Christians we hear of conversions marked by clear repentance, a conviction of the truth from reading the Bible, an encounter with the Living Lord Jesus, or a touch of the Holy Spirit which changed their lives. Conversions to Islam have very different features.

Our Muslim friends need to understand that no one is born a Christian but rather, that we are all born with the capacity to sin. Most Muslims struggle with the concept of 'original sin', although they will concede that all people sin at some point. The Qur'an describes the ongoing struggle human beings have with sin and its consequences (Q 7:19-43), which is hard to reconcile if Islam has no 'original sin'. Jesus said, "You must be born again" (John 3:7). John 3:16-17 tells us that God sent His Son into the world to save us from the consequences of sin, as only God can truly save. Deep down, most religious people will acknowledge that salvation only comes from God, despite their good-works based religions. This gives you a chance to tell your story of how you became a Christian, and your growing relationship with the Living Lord Jesus.

'What made you decide Islam is true?'

The answer to this question will help you to understand the extent to which your friend has assessed the truth claims of Islam, and what reasons are important to them. You could ask the question in different forms such as, 'Have you ever considered that Islam might not be true? or 'Why do you think Islam is true?' or 'What do you think are the most important reasons for believing in Islam?' On the other hand, your questions could be focused on Muhammad: 'Why do you think Muhammad was a prophet of god?' This question should lead to an opportunity for you to explain who Jesus is and why you believe Christianity to be true. Here, you may wish to talk about the resurrection, your favourite evidence for Christianity, how Jesus has transformed your life, or why you do not fear death. Be honest and real.

'What does it mean to be a Muslim?'

This question should enable your friends to clarify their understanding of Islam, whilst creating an opportunity for you, in turn, to explain what it means to be a Christian. Conversations with Muslim friends can sometimes be one-sided, especially if you come from a 'turn-taking'[13] culture or have been raised not to interrupt someone mid-speech. Most of our Muslim friends do not have this as part of their way of interacting, unless they were born and raised in Western cultures. The wonderful reality for the Christian is the commissioning from the Lord Jesus Himself to "go out into all the world, making disciples of all nations, baptising in the Name of the Father, Son and Holy Spirit" (Matthew 28:19), which means we are called to tell others what it means to be a Christian, and ask our friends to consider it.

'What do you think God is like?'

When life is easy, many people tend not reflect on this question. However, when the world struggles or faces uncertain times, this becomes especially important.

Be prepared for the Trinity to come up at some point. Be aware that some Muslims[14] have been coached in three areas of discussion with Christians: (1) the divinity of Jesus (2) the Trinity and (3) the reliability of the Bible. Muslims will often turn conversations towards their perceived 'problems' with the Bible and Biblical theology. We encourage you to continue to hold Islam accountable throughout your discussions, and to ensure that both religions are examined – not just Christianity, especially when it comes to who God is, and what God is like.[15] The character of Allah is very different from the character of God – the latter being fundamentally triune, relational, loving and victorious over evil.

Many Muslims living in nations they perceive to be 'Christian' will adopt a view of Allah that is closer to the Christian perception of the God of the Bible. So, some may claim that Allah is loving, Allah is near,[16] and that Allah will save them. Before any response is given, it is helpful to ask your Muslim friend where such ideas are found in the Qur'an. Some may refer to the often quoted Qur'anic statement, 'Allah is merciful and compassionate.' (Q 1:1) This claim is made without any examples of how Allah has been merciful or compassionate. Questions can be asked about these statements, especially as many are not supported by Allah's actions or direct commands. Allah is very different from the relational Biblical God.

The Lord Jesus is just, merciful and loving. This is seen right through the pages of the Bible. Where in the Qur'an are these essential core characteristics evidenced? It turns out that these are Christian concepts, because the Qur'an has no clear theology of Allah loving all people, and proving that love by dying for them. Allah certainly never chose to die for people, nor does Allah serve people, whilst God, revealed through the Bible, came to serve humanity through Jesus (Exodus 13:21; Isaiah 53; John 13:1-17) and proved how He values us by taking the punishment for our sins – in our place.

A Muslim may respond that this would not befit Allah. In contrast, thank the Lord God who saw it fitting to sacrifice His life – to give us eternal life.

'What do you think Christians believe?'

This is a great way to find out how much your Muslim friends understand about Christianity, and to be clear on any misunderstandings or misconceptions they might have. Try to challenge these misconceptions. Christians are to be people of truth, and being truthful includes challenging false ideas circulating about Christianity and Islam.

'What does Allah think about you?'

Most Muslims won't know what Allah thinks of them. Their position is as slaves to Allah, not as children. They will hope that Allah will look favourably on them but will not have more assurance than that. Christians, by contrast, have reason to be confident on the basis of God's promises that they are God's children. He has proven His care for humanity (Isaiah 53; John 3:14-18), by acting to rescue us (Hebrews 11-12:3).

How does Allah show his love for you?'

You may want to ask, 'Where in the Qur'an does it say that Allah loves everyone?' The answer is: *nowhere*. You will also need to press home the question, 'In what way has Allah demonstrated his love for human beings?' You can share your own experience of God's care, but more importantly, talk of Jesus' death on the cross and His power to rise again – which only God could do. John 3:16 is an apt verse to quote. You could then ask about Allah's mercy. Islam proclaims that Allah is merciful to slaves (Q 15:49)[17] and forgives all sins (Q 39:53).[18] Hence, 'How has Allah shown mercy to you?' Questions probing Allah's justice and the basis on which Allah can forgive sins could lead to helpful conversations about the cross, and the death and resurrection of the Lord Jesus.

'What do you think of sects or groups within Islam?'

This will enable you to understand how sectarian your friend is. You can explain what you think about different Christian denominations but do emphasise that we are united on one core element – the deity, death and resurrection of Jesus. You may need to talk about cults and sectarian groups that deny the divinity of Jesus, and why their beliefs are not Biblical. (See the positive affirmation of Jesus' deity in Colossians 1:15-20).

'How does prayer work for you?'

This is a question to bring in the reality of relationship with God. Most Muslims do not think that Christians pray very much, or are surprised that we are happy to pray anywhere at any time, and in any language. Islamic prayer is highly ritualised and public, in direct contrast to Matthew 6:5-8. It is an act of obedience, an act of worship, and a way to try to appease Allah. It is done as a slave to a master, not as a child to a loving, perfect Father. Some Muslims believe they can pray personal prayers after the ritual prayers have been completed. This can be a helpful area to pursue. 'Does – or can – Allah hear you? If he does, does it mean Allah is then like us or even subservient to our requests? How does Allah hear you? Does Allah self-reveal to Muslims?'

Emphasise that Christian prayer is a conversation with God. It includes worship, thanksgiving for His daily provision and for answered prayer, and also repentance, confession, supplication, intercession, and personal communion. Primarily, Christian prayer is communication between God's children and their loving Heavenly Father.

'What is worship in Islam?'

Worship in Islam is quite different from worship in Christianity. Muslims have a concept called *Deen* – a way of life and practice that includes prayers, almsgiving, pilgrimages, fasting and repetition of the statement of faith, that please Allah and hopefully grant them blessings and eternal reward. It is wrapped up largely in the main pillars and rituals of obedience. Prayer, for example, is an act of worship – submission to Allah and Allah's laws. Our

Muslim friends would understand that people's lives should reflect their beliefs. However, worshipping Allah looks very different from worshipping the Lord God.

A Christian is called to live a holy life of worship. Everything we do and say should show our love for the Lord, and be offered as a 'sacrifice of praise' to Him (Hebrews 13:15), which means openly professing God's name. We are called to worship in 'spirit and truth' (John 4:23-24), which is one of the reasons why we need to ask probing questions to challenge false opinions of the Lord God. Whatever we do, we must do for the glory of God (1 Corinthians 10:23-31; Colossians 3:17). We are to sing His praises (Psalm 63:5; Psalm 150; Hebrews 13:15), meditate on His Word throughout the day (Psalm 1:2), and yearn for and seek Him (Psalm 42:1). We are called to live holy lives (Leviticus 11:44; 1 Peter 1:16). In a nutshell, our lives must be an act of worship that shows our love for and relationship with the Lord God.

Do you pray five times a day?'

This is one of the five pillars (practices) of Islam. You will understand how serious your friends' faith is from their answers to this question. If they say they do pray five times a day, you could ask where that is commanded in the Qur'an. In fact, the command to pray five times a day is not found in the Qur'an. Only three prayers are listed. To understand how to practise the ritualised prayers of Islam, Muslims have to refer to texts outside the Qur'an, such as the Islamic law or traditions.

You could also ask them why they pray. Ask if they prefer the ritual prayer or the private prayer that can be said once their ritual prayers are over. Explain that Christians have direct access to God. The curtain being torn from top to bottom when Jesus died on the cross (Matthew 27:51) is an excellent picture to aid our Muslim friends to understand how we can enter directly into God's presence – a great bridge to the Gospel.

'How can I pray for you today?'

Offer to pray there and then. Most Muslims will not turn you down, and you may be surprised at what God will do! As a precaution, do not, for example, *promise* healing, but do *pray* for healing, if that is the felt need. Always pray in Jesus' name (John 14:13; Colossians 3:17), explaining to your friend beforehand, that this is how God hears our prayers. If they refuse prayer, then we must not insist on praying for them then and there. We can always pray for them privately, in our own time.

'Do you know God's forgiveness?'

Muslims are not confident of their salvation. Even Muhammad was not confident that he had received forgiveness, or what his state would be in the afterlife. In the Qur'an Muhammad states, "I am not something original among the messengers, nor do I know what will be done with me or with you" (Q 46:9 Sahih International).

The Qur'an presents a mixed view of how to escape judgment. A read through of the Qur'an will show that this is not clear. Islam has only laws and regulations to follow, with no assurance of salvation.

Romans 8:3 explains that God's law cannot save: 'For what the law could not do ... God did by sending His own Son ...'. The question provides an opportunity to talk about your experience of forgiveness, assurance of salvation and communion with the Lord God (John 3:16; Acts 4:12; Romans 8:38-39). In contrast, it is important to remember that there is no clear concept of salvation in Islam. Ultimately, Islam offers only a garden after death in which, from a Biblical perspective, much sin dwells, and Allah is not present (Q 37:40-49, Q43:70-71, Q55:54-78).[19]

'Do you know if you will be with God when you die?'

This is a very important question because Muslims will never live with or talk with Allah, according to their own theology. Allah does not reside in the paradise, or the garden that the Qur'an talks about. According to the Qur'an, Muslims may see Allah on Judgment Day (Q 75:22-23), but there will be no interaction or relationship. Islam has no concept of the God who walks and talks with us, as seen throughout the Bible (Genesis 3:8-9; Isaiah 7:14; Matthew 1:21-23; Revelation 21:3-6). If your friend responds, "Yes, I will be with God", ask if that means they will literally walk and talk with Allah. Expect them to say, "No". If they say, "Yes, I will be with Allah", ask for a Qur'anic verse that supports this notion. Probe their thoughts further on the matter: "You mean you will sit, and see, and talk and walk with Allah?" You then have an opportunity to introduce them to the relational God with whom Christians commune, who will one day live with them and personally take away their pain, so there will be 'no more death, nor sorrow, nor crying … [and] no more pain, for the former things have passed away' (Revelation 21:4).

Is God personal?

Is He personal to you? Do you have a personal relationship with God? Would you like to? These are key questions to ask, because according to Islamic theology, Allah does not directly engage with human beings. Explore how a Muslim interacts with and communes with God, because there is a lack of relationship between Allah and those who worship him. That is not to say Muslims do not have religious experiences – they do – but does that mean that Allah interacts on a human level, and isn't that "unbefitting" of a deity in Islamic theology?

'What difference does your faith make to your life?'

We hope that it is making a difference in your own life! A Muslim may have a misguided notion that Christianity is only a private, Sunday religion. Ensure that they know it is not, and why.

'Does Ramadan bring lasting change to your life?'

Muslims fast from dawn to dusk during Ramadan. In fact, significantly more food is consumed by Muslims at the time of Ramadan during the night hours.[20] What is the lasting spiritual effect? Why do they fast? Compare this with the Bible's view of fasting. Jesus' own words in Matthew 6:5-18 are a powerful antidote to the Islamic concept of external rules and rituals, including the fast. Jesus' Sermon on the Mount is our answer to Islamic theology on many levels. Isaiah 58:3-9 and Matthew 6:16-18 provides a form of fasting that Muslims need to hear about. These verses challenge the heart of Islamic rituals.

A Muslim might point to the law of 'right intention' in Islamic law manuals, outlined in detail as an element of the practices they must accomplish. Even the concept of 'right intentions' is presented as forms of law which can be broken. What is significant is how those laws do not reflect the deep relationship, communion and trust that is at the heart of Biblical law.

'If you found Christianity to be true, would you become a Christian?'[21]

The emphasis here is on the truth. How committed is your friend to believing what is true? Are they more committed to their culture and religion than to what is true? If Jesus, who gave up everything for us, and is the way, the truth and the life, are we willing to give up everything for Him? This is a tough ask. For some of our friends, turning to Jesus could mean losing family, or even this physical life. That is why we must be clear in presenting Jesus – His beauty, His gift of salvation and what salvation ultimately means: forgiveness of past sins, the presence of the Holy Spirit to lead us in the right way, and eternal life with the Lord Jesus, transcending this life.

'Have you read any of the New Testament?'

The New Testament is called the *Injil* by Muslims, although Muslims will claim that the original *Injil*, to which the Qur'an refers (Q 5:46, 57:27), has been lost. Consequently, Muslims have only the Bible to find out about Jesus. Do encourage your friends to read it or offer to read it with them, starting perhaps, with John's Gospel. For a response to the commonly used Islamic claim of New Testament corruption, see 'Questions Muslims Ask' (pp 109ff).

'What does Allah think of me?'

In your Muslim friend's eyes you are an unbeliever, worthy of judgment since you are not a Muslim. So, you could ask, 'What is your attitude towards me as an unbeliever?' 'How can Allah forgive me?', 'Where do I stand before Allah as far as judgment is concerned?' and 'What good news do you have for me as a non-Muslim?' Then follow up with Sura 9 in the Qur'an which has a number of verses commanding Muslims to wage war on unbelievers (Q 9:5, 29, 111, 123).[22] What do you feel about that?' For more on this topic, see 'Questions on Violence' (pp 87ff).

You could also ask, 'How has Allah proved his love for you as a Muslim, and for me as a non-Muslim?' The Bible has numerous illustrations which show us that love is demonstrated in the way we live and relate to others (James 2:14-26; 1 John 4:18). The God of the Bible clearly shows that His love can be experienced. (Jeremiah 31:2-3; Micah 6:6-8; John 3:16; Romans 5:8). But what about Allah? Can you experience Allah's love? If so, then how?

'Would you read and let me know what you think of this book?'
Some of your friends might be willing to read a book you recommend. We suggest *Seeking Allah, Finding Jesus* by Nabeel Qureshi. In the recommended resources section there are some other books you could also suggest. It is important that the books you recommend are ones you have read yourself.

3

Questions comparing Jesus and Muhammad

Questions about Muhammad can be a very sensitive area for Muslims, more so than about Allah or the Qur'an. We can see this in the violent responses some Muslims have to cartoons and critique of Muhammad.

Some people ask questions just to provoke. We are not interested in provoking or insulting someone for the sake of it. We, however, are interested in healthy discussions and asking questions that help people to reconsider their position, and consider Jesus instead. It is this which is at the heart of the following questions.

'What has Muhammad done for you?'
This provides an opportunity for you to discuss what Jesus has done for you. Don't be shy of giving your own honest assessment of Muhammad as well.

'Is Muhammad alive today?'
Muslims claim that Muhammad's tomb in Medina can be visited.[23] But Jesus is no longer in a tomb. He is alive (Mark 16:6).

'What do you know about Jesus?'
The answer to this open-ended question will help you understand what your friend thinks and knows about Jesus. Your friend may say that they respect Jesus and revere Him as a prophet. You could then ask what practical steps they have taken in respecting Him. Have they attempted to find out more about Him, or read any accounts about Him in the Bible? Have they read the Gospels? Have they considered His work through history – from creation (Genesis 1-3; John 1; Colossians 1:15; Hebrews 1:1-3) through to when He will return (Revelation 19)? What do they make of His conversation with the Heavenly Father: "...glorify me with the glory I had with you before the world began" (John 17:5)?

'Have you ever compared the lives and actions of Muhammad and the Lord Jesus?'[24]

In this section is a helpful comparison between Jesus and Muhammad, with references from the Bible, the Qur'an, the Sira[25] (biography), the Hadith (sayings and actions of Muhammad), and Tarikh (history from Islamic tradition) to support the claims made.

Jesus	Muhammad
Born of a virgin (Matthew 1:18-25; Isaiah 7:14)	Born normally (Sira pp.68-69)[26]
Deep Biblical knowledge (Luke 2:39-52)	"Unlettered" (illiterate) of a pagan family (Q 7:157-158; Sira pp.37-38, Buk. V1 bk1 h3)[27]
Holy One from Heaven (Daniel 7:13-14; John 6:38; Revelation 1:12-19)	Just a prophet; not sure if he or who will go to paradise (Q 7:188; 46:9)
Poor; nowhere to lay His head (Luke 9:58)	Took 20% loot for himself and his family (Sira p.466; Q 8:41; 48:20)
Miracles over creation, life and death (John 11:43-44; Mark 3:9-11; Mark 4:39)	Performed no miracles nor prophesied (Q 6:37; 13:7; 29:50)
Made blind eyes see (Luke 18:35-43; John 9)	Made seeing eyes blind (Buk. V7 b71 h590)[28]
Had the power to forgive sins and make the lame walk (Matthew 9:2-8)	Made the walking lame (Buk. 7:71:590; 2:24:577)[29]
Healed withered hands (Matthew 12:10-13; Mark 3:1-6)	Cut off hands for being Muhammad's enemy (Q 5:33) or for stealing (Buk. V4 bk 52 h261)[30]
Taught faithful, monogamous marriage (Matthew 19:4-9)	Taught and practised polygamy, as encouraged by Allah (Q 4:3; 66:1-5)
Raised the dead (Mark 5:21-43; John 11:1-57)	Taught to kill the living, as directed by Allah (Q 5:33; 47:4; 5:9,29, Sira p. 308)
Is our Creator (John 1:3; Colossians 1:16; Hebrews 1:10)	Is created (Sira p. 68-69)
Forgave his opponents (Matthew 5:44; Luke 23:34,43; John 3:16-17)	Had his opponents killed (Q 4:89; 8:12-13; 9:5,29; 47:4)
Set the condemned free (John 8:1-11; Isaiah 61:1-3)	Enslaved the free (Q 4:24; 33:50; Sira p. 466)
Was sinless (Hebrews 4:15; 1 Peter 1:15-16)	Was sinful (Q 47:19;[31] 48:1-2 — to ask forgiveness suggests that sin has been committed)
Jesus knew what would happen to Him after His death (Mark 10:32-34)	Was unsure what would happen to him after death (Q 46:9; Buk. V5 bk58 h266)[32]

Jesus	Muhammad
Died for sinners (John 1:29; 10:11)	Had sinners killed (Q 9:5; 47:4)
Was crucified (Matthew 27:35)	Crucified others according to Allah's command (Q 5:33; Dawud bk38 h4339)[33]
Rose from the dead (Luke 24; Revelation 2:8)	Is not alive but is buried in Medina (Buk. V3 bk48 h848; V4 bk56 h660;[34] Sira p. 683; Al-Tabari v9 p. 208)[35]

'Why was Isa born of a virgin and Muhammad wasn't?'

The Bible teaches that Mary was a virgin when Jesus was conceived by the power of the Holy Spirit (Matt 1:18-21; Luke 1:26-38). Interestingly, the Qur'an asserts that Isa, who many Muslims believe to be Jesus, was also born of a virgin (Q 19:20) after the angel Gabriel blew into her to make her pregnant (Q 21:91). This indicates that Isa's birth was miraculous, whereas Muhammad's birth was not. Doesn't this mean that Isa is unique, and far more significant than Muhammad? Yet, even this man, Isa, cannot live up to the life, actions and eternality of Jesus.

We love to share with our Muslim friends the hundreds of prophecies that foretell the arrival of the Holy One from Heaven. The virgin birth in Biblical teaching points to the promised arrival of God coming to live with us. For example, consider the prophecy of Isaiah 7:14. Here Isaiah tells us that the virgin shall conceive,[36] and bear a Son and shall call His name Immanuel – meaning God with us. God was to be with us in human form.[37] This prophecy was fulfilled seven hundred years later, and is described in Matthew 1:21-23:

> "And she will bring forth a Son, and you shall call His name JESUS [meaning God saves], for He will save His people from their sins." So, all this was done that it might be fulfilled which was spoken by the Lord through the prophet, saying, 'Behold, the virgin shall be with child, and bear a Son, and they shall call His name Immanuel,' which is translated, 'God with us'.

'Isn't it interesting that Jesus demonstrated extraordinary spiritual knowledge even as a child?'

Spiritual knowledge is revered in Islam. Jesus was able to challenge the religious teachers even when He was a child (Luke 2:39-52). The child Isa in the Qur'an is a remarkable person compared with Muhammad, and while he is no competition for the historical Jesus, comparing the three of them can lead to fascinating discussions. According to the Qur'an, Isa – who Muslims believe to be Jesus[38] – could speak as a baby (Q 3:46; 19:29-33).[39]

Muhammad had a fairly normal upbringing, living as his culture and developing ideology dictated. An important question we need to consider is why or how Jesus knew so much as a child – so much so that he shocked religious leaders who saw His authority and understanding (Luke 2:41-48). In contrast, Muhammad's first experiences were typically pagan in nature. Take, for example, the unusual story of his heart being washed by angels, or his confusion about which spiritual being was speaking to him in a cave – an angel or Satan[40] – or the manifestations (fainting,[41] sweating,[42] difficulty in speaking[43] and hallucinating[44]) when he received spiritual verses. To the Christian mind, the big question we are left with is: who was Muhammad communing with? If it wasn't the Living God, who was it?

These questions can be difficult for Muslims to answer, partly due to how the evidence of Muhammad's life points away from an experience with the Living God. Quite often a Muslim will point you to their Imam, or the religious leaders (Ulema), to answer your questions with the caveat, "I'm not a scholar." It is helpful to encourage our Muslim friends to see the importance of investigating our respective faiths for themselves, if they are truly concerned about knowing the right way.

Shouldn't we all be concerned about discovering the truth, especially about the founder of the religion to which we have committed ourselves?

'Why are Muhammad's spiritual and life experiences so pagan in nature?'

If you are familiar with the Bible you will recognise immediately how Muhammad's life, experiences and teaching stand against the Lord God. It is instructive to consider Muhammad's life and teaching in the light of two Bible passages: one from the book of Exodus, namely, the Ten Commandments (Exodus 20), and the other, from the Sermon on the Mount (Matthew 5-7).

The entire Bible challenges the behaviour, beliefs and claims of Muhammad. Here are some verses to begin the comparison: Hebrews 10:26-31 (judgment for rejecting the Son), Deuteronomy 18:20-22 (prophets who do not speak for the LORD), Isaiah 5:20 (those who call evil good), Jeremiah 23:16 (false prophets), Mark 7:6-9 (man-made rules), 2 Peter 2:1 (false prophets), and 1 John 4:1-6 (spirit of the Antichrist; spirit of error). The starting point is Jesus. Whoever claims to be a prophet, yet rejects the divinity of Jesus, cannot be of God. Jesus said, "I am the way, the truth, and the life. No one comes to the Father except through Me" (John 14:6).

See the question, *'By what authority does Muhammad speak?'* on page 59.

'Does it bother you that Jesus performed multiple miracles whereas Muhammad didn't perform any?'

What does this convey about the status of Jesus vis-a-vis Muhammad?

We know from the Gospels that Jesus performed numerous miracles. Many people mistakenly believe that He performed miracles only when He walked amongst men two thousand years ago, and forget who created the world – King Jesus! (John 1; Colossians 1; Hebrews 1). What is more, Jesus worked miracle after miracle as recorded right through the Scriptures.

The Qur'an says that the man Isa (whom Muslims claim is Jesus) performed healing miracles (Q 3:49). By contrast, Muhammad performed no miracles, although Muslims will point to what they claim is 'the miracle of the Qur'an'. For more on this, see chapter 5 on questions about the Qur'an. According to the Qur'an, the only miracle that Muhammad performed was the revelation of the Qur'an.[45]

> And those who disbelieved say, 'Why has a sign not been sent down to him from his Lord?' (Q 13:7 Sahih International).

And again:

> But they say, 'Why are not signs sent down to him from his Lord?' Say, 'The signs are only with Allah, and I am only a clear warner'. And is it not sufficient for them that We revealed to you the Book which is recited to them? Indeed in that is a mercy and reminder for a people who believe (Q 29:50-51 Sahih International).

This last verse teaches the sufficiency of the Qur'an while exempting Muhammad from having to perform any miracles. Yet if the Qur'an were sufficient, why are so many other books, in addition to the Qur'an, needed to teach Muslims how to live their lives? [46]

'Since Jesus performed numerous miracles, doesn't that mean He is a better representative* of God?'

Some Muslims may point to a strange verse in Q 54:1-2 about the moon being split in two. While the verse is speaking about a future event, many say Muhammad actually performed this miracle, based on traditions in the Hadith. If so, it can be helpful to ask why no one in the 7th century noticed that the moon had been split in two. Surely scientists today would be able to test if this were true. But even if Muhammad did split the moon, this 'miracle' appears to lack any purpose. Compare this with the miracles of Jesus, who calmed a storm to save lives (Matthew 8:23-27), fed thousands of people with just five loaves of bread and two fish (Matthew 14:13-21) and healed people of every kind of sickness and disease (Matthew 4:23). What was the purpose of Muhammad splitting the moon?

The topic of miracles can be helpful to lead our Muslim friends back to hearing about Jesus' work throughout history.

*The Bible doesn't just say that Jesus is a representative. It says that He is the 'image' of God (Colossians 1:15) and that all the fullness of deity is in Him (Numbers 12:8; Colossians 2:9). No wonder that He could perform the miracles that He did.

'Why, according to the Qur'an, is Isa sinless, while Muhammad was not?'

The Bible teaches that Jesus was sinless (2 Corinthians 5:21; Hebrews 4:15; 1 John 3:5) – a wonderful truth since only God is sinless.

The Qur'an teaches that there was a 'holy/righteous son' (Q 19:19 Yusuf Ali/ Muhsin Khan), or 'pure boy' (Sahih International); the name given to him is Isa (Q 19:34). Whilst Isa cannot be Jesus, Isa's 'righteousness' is significant because only God is righteous. Simple logic leads us to ask if the Qur'an is saying that Isa is God? This can lead to more questions on the topic, such as: 'Is God holy?' What does it mean to call God holy? Can people be holy too, and if they are holy, does this mean they are like God?

Christ crucified is 'folly' to the Muslims, not just because the Bible warns us that this is so (1 Corinthians 1:23; 1 Peter 2:8),[47] but because the Qur'an replaces Jesus with Isa, just as it has replaced the God of the Bible with Allah.

Muhammad was far from sinless, as even a cursory examination of his life will show. The Qur'an informs us that Muhammad is commanded by Allah to ask forgiveness for his sin: "So know [O Muhammad] that there is no deity except Allah and ask for forgiveness for your sins ..." (Q 47:19 Sahih International). See also Q 48:1-2, which points to Muhammad's past and future sins.

Since the Qur'an records a sinless person called Isa, the superiority of Isa's character and actions in the Qur'an compared with those of Muhammad (Q 3:46, 49) provides a link to explore someone better than Muhammad. Remember those helpful comparisons of Jesus, Isa and Muhammad in conversations with Muslim friends.[48] Ultimately, we need to move them away from Isa (whose existence in the Qur'an serves to deny the divinity of Jesus) and back to the Biblical Jesus.

To help your friends truly grasp truth, always move away from the Qur'an and to the Bible.

'Why do Muslims call themselves "Slaves of Allah" (Abdullah) when Jesus sets us free from slavery?'

At this point, we suggest that you introduce your Muslim friends to the message of the whole Bible – freedom from enslavement to sin (Isaiah 61:1-3; John 8: 31-36), relationship with God (John 15:15), and the value of all human beings (Genesis 1:27-28; Psalm 139:13-16; Galatians 3:28-29).

You have an opportunity to introduce them to the concepts of freedom from enslavement to sin, from physical enslavement, and enslavement to man-made religious laws.[49] Christians, having been set free from slavery to sin, become voluntary slaves of God out of love and appreciation for what He has done for them (Romans 6:20-22).

A follow-up question about Muhammad's slaves usually surprises Muslims, as many are not aware that Muhammad had slaves. As an example, Muhammad was given freedom by Allah to own women ("what your right hands possess" – Q 33:50). Parts of this topic are covered in questions on slavery (pp 53ff), and the section, 'Questions on Women in Islam' (pp 79ff).

'Why was Isa taken up to heaven, but not Muhammad?'

The Qur'an teaches that Isa was raised up to Allah (Q 4:157-158). In contrast, Muhammad was not raised up to Allah. Surely, this makes Isa more authoritative than Muhammad. Jesus, by contrast, did not merely rise from the dead. He ascended in the presence of witnesses (Luke 24: 50-52; Acts 1:1-11) to rule in authority (Psalm 24; Daniel 7:9-14; Hebrews 12:2; Revelation 5). Since Jesus is alive, He can hear our prayers, but Muhammad is not alive, which means he cannot hear anyone's prayers.[50]

'Why is Jesus coming back, but not Muhammad?'

Christians know that Jesus is coming back to be the judge of all the nations, and destroy sin once and for all (Revelation 19). Muslims believe that Isa will return to earth in the end times. The return of Isa is mentioned in the Qur'an:

> And (Jesus)[51] shall be a Sign (for the coming of) the Hour (of Judgment) ... (Q 43:61 Yusuf Ali).

The return of Isa is much more explicit in several Hadith.

> How will you be when the son of Mary (i.e. Jesus)[52] descends amongst you and your imam is among you? (Bukhari V4 bk55 h658).[53]

> Allah's Messenger said, 'By Him in Whose Hands my soul is, son of Mary (Jesus) will shortly descend amongst you people (Muslims) as a just ruler and will break the Cross and kill the pig and abolish the Jizya (a tax taken from the non-Muslims, who are in the protection of the Muslim government). Then there will be abundance of money and nobody will accept charitable gifts (Bukhari V3 bk34 h425).[54]

But Muhammad is supposed to be the final prophet, so why is it that Isa is coming back and not Muhammad? What is more, why is there an antichrist (the Dajjal) figure in Islamic tradition, but not an anti-Muhammad?

'Consider Jesus who never murdered anyone, whereas Muhammad had many killed.'

Jesus is 'the Alpha and the Omega' (Revelation 1:8) and the 'author of life' (Acts 3:15 NIV). During His 33 years on earth He did not take a single life. In fact, He sometimes brought people back to life! John 10:10 tells us clearly that Jesus came to give life. His life was an example to us of a perfect life. Yet, we cannot forget that Jesus is also King and Judge over us all (Revelation 19:11-16), but while He has judged and will judge, He does not murder.

Some Muslim friends may point you to the 'violence' of Jesus in John 2:13-17 (cf. Matthew 21:12-13) where Jesus drove out the merchants in the temple. John 2:16-17 show Jesus' righteous anger towards corruption of true religion in the temple. Seeing people robbed of their few possessions through false religion, and God's house being turned into 'a den of thieves', Jesus turns the tables upside down, using a whip to drive out the thieves.[55] This was righteous anger – something even sinful human beings should understand. Even we, in our brokenness, understand when deep injustices and evil take place. How much more, then, God Himself?

Others may claim that Jesus advocated violence in Luke 19:27: "But bring here those enemies of mine, who did not want me to reign over them, and slay them before me." This verse is usually presented out of context without recognition that it is in a parable which begins at verse 11. The words are from the mouth of the nobleman in the parable – a story that Jesus is telling about a future event, as a warning. This story was told to people near Jerusalem, who believed that the Kingdom of God was near. Jesus was getting people ready for judgment day, when He would judge the living and the dead. Yet many ignore His Kingship though He wants us to take this seriously. We understand this for our own societies, where the law of the land, the rule of the leader, is to be taken seriously (Romans 13). Our Muslim friends understand this concept well, and it can be refreshing to discuss these matters of being ready for 'that day' with them. However, Islam has denied Jesus, His suffering for us (Psalm 22; Isaiah 53) and the salvation He offers, which means that Muslims are not ready, in the Lord's eyes, to meet Him. If we love our friends we will introduce them to the true, Living Lord Jesus who reigns at the right hand of the Father (Psalm 24:7; Psalm 110:1; Philippians 2:9-11; Hebrews 1:13). This parable, in context, far from advocating violence, is referring to future judgment.

Another verse that Muslims sometimes use to argue that Jesus advocated violence, is Matthew 10:34: "Do not think that I came to bring peace on earth. I did not come to bring peace but a sword." Jesus is saying that belief in Him can cause enmity between family members and friends, including murder against those who trust in Jesus. Islamic law, in demanding the death penalty for those who leave Islam, shows how the words of Jesus came to pass. Furthermore, and generally speaking, Christians who have left the faith of their family to follow the Lord Jesus, are often threatened and disowned by their family members. Matthew 10:34 states that choosing Jesus is costly. See also Matthew 16:24-26.

The above verses also challenge us to see where our true devotion lies. Do we love Jesus even more than we love our family or our friends? Do we love God as much as He loves us? Do we long to live with God and see Him face to face? Is Jesus our joy? Do we believe He is enough to satisfy us and lead us through the darkest times? Do we really know Him? Do we really trust Him? He gave up His life to save us. Would we give up ours to rescue others?

Muhammad, by contrast, when he stood as judge over unbelievers, was not judging sin or corrupt religion. Rather, he was a man who affirmed the killing of those who stood against him and his men.[56] He was a warrior who fought in many battles. One such battle was with the Jewish Banu Qurayza tribe, which can be found in Ibn Ishaq's biography of Muhammad and his followers. After the battle of the trench, he had between 600-900[57] men from that tribe beheaded.[58] He fought in numerous other battles and personally ordered or supported the killing of many people.[59]

Jesus, by contrast, told Peter to put away his sword, and healed the High Priest's servant, whose ear Peter had cut off (Luke 22:49-51). Rather than retaliating when violence was committed against Him, He cried out, "Father, forgive them" (Luke 23:34). This part of His eternal ministry was to give His life in order to rescue humanity from a horrific eternity separated from Himself.

Consider Jesus as 'the Alpha and the Omega' (Revelation 1:8), the One who has authority over life and death – the great Judge before whom we will all stand one day (2 Corinthians 5:10). He judges rightly, and He does not randomly kill.

Jesus died for His enemies. Muhammad killed his enemies.

'Did you know that Jesus never owned slaves, but that Muhammad owned and distributed slaves?'

Muhammad took slaves as war booty and traded slaves. Here is an example from the Hadith:

> There came a slave and pledged allegiance to Allah's Apostle (may peace be upon him) on migration [sic]; he

(the Holy Prophet) did not know that he was a slave. Then there came his master and demanded him back, whereupon Allah's Apostle (may peace be upon him) said: 'Sell him to me.' And he bought him for two black slaves, and he did not afterwards take allegiance from anyone until he had asked him whether he was a slave (or a free man) (Sahih Muslim, Book 10, Hadith 3901[60] or Hadith 1602).[61]

Muhammad traded in black slaves and sex slaves, as we see in the many references to the slaves of Muhammad, his family and his men.[62] We know that Islam spread through North Africa into Spain by 711 AD.[63] Its conquests were accomplished through the enslavement of North Africans, who were brought into Europe as slave-warriors. The conquests of North Africa, soon after Islam's inception, began one thousand four hundred years of trans-Saharan slave trade at the hands of Muslim rulers.[64]

Jesus never owned slaves. He categorically stood against slavery. The Bible reminds us of His work in history to rescue people from slavery, both spiritual (Isaiah 61:1-3) and physical (Exodus 20:2; Philemon), pointing out His rescue of His people from slavery in Egypt under the Pharaohs.

The New Testament writers exhort new believers in Jesus, some of whom were slave owners and others slaves, to see each other as brothers, not as slave and master (Philemon verse 16). The Bible calls us all to serve one another, to see the other as better than ourselves, and to love our neighbour as ourselves (Galatians 5:13). Jesus has always been the One who came to set prisoners free (Isaiah 61:1-3). He came to serve and calls us to be willing to lay down our lives for others (1 John 3:16). The Bible does not call us to enslave others. Galatians 3:28 sums up our standing before Jesus: 'There is neither Jew nor Greek, there is neither slave nor free, there is neither male nor female; for you are all one in Christ Jesus.' This is why Biblically literate Christians have been behind abolition movements.

Some will point to a couple of verses in the Bible which, in modern translations, seem to give support to slavery. Yet, this is far from the truth. There are certainly examples in the Bible of people becoming indentured servants (working to pay off debt), and in times of war there is the conquering of people. However, the Lord God holds everyone to account. We see this in how God's people, who were chosen to be His witnesses, were also exiled and at times enslaved, usually after immense evil existed among them, and after hundreds of years of patience and warning from the Lord. The Bible also reports times of slavery, simply due to the hardened hearts of evil rulers. Slavery is a sure sign of the evil of human beings. A Saviour from all slavery is needed. This is at the heart of Biblical teaching.

Imposing a modern-day view of slavery onto Bible passages does not do justice to what actually happened in ancient history. We also cannot compare the Trans-Saharan, Viking, Pan-African, Transatlantic and Ottoman slave trades, to name a few, with indentured servanthood in Biblical times. We must face the horrific nature of the Trans-Saharan and Transatlantic slavery through to the Ottoman Imperial Harem slave houses. Healing from the memory of these can only become reality when we enjoy the freedom that only Jesus can give (Isaiah 61:1-3; John 8:32).

What is troubling about Islam is how Islamic slavery (which is taught in all its main texts, especially the capture of women and girls and the murder of their men) supports this evil which God constantly stands against through His Scriptures. Consider this: 'He who kidnaps a man and sells him, or if he is found in his hand, shall surely be put to death' (Exodus 21:16). The same punishment goes for those who rape – this would include the rape of a woman from a nation just conquered in battle (Deuteronomy 22:25). God takes enslavement and rape very seriously.

'Why is Muhammad not prophesied in the Bible?'

The Qur'an claims that Muhammad is prophesied in the Bible:

> Those who follow the Messenger, the unlettered prophet, whom they find written in what they have of the Torah and the Gospel, ... (Q 7:157 Sahih International).[65]

> And [mention] when Jesus, the son of Mary, said, "O children of Israel, indeed I am the messenger of Allah to you confirming what came before me of the Torah and bringing good tidings of a messenger to come after

me, whose name is Ahmad." But when he came to them with clear evidences, they said, "This is obvious magic" (Q 61:6 Sahih International).

In this verse, Isa employs the diminutive form of Muhammad's name, 'Ahmad', saying that he is coming after him – a verse used by Muslims as proof that Muhammad is prophesied in the teaching of Isa.

To be clear, there are no prophecies relating to Muhammad in the Bible, whereas there are many that relate to Jesus' birth, death and resurrection.

To find Muhammad in the Bible, Muslims will usually point to Deuteronomy:

> *I will raise up for them a Prophet like you from among their brethren, and I will put My words in His mouth ...* (Deuteronomy 18:18).

The Islamic argument goes like this: 'brethren' refers to the brothers of the Israelites, who are the Ishmaelites – the line from which Muslims believe Muhammad came.[66]

This argument does not stand, because 'brethren' is just a way of saying 'fellow believers' or 'community'. The same terminology is used in Deuteronomy 17:15, which clearly shows that 'brethren' means Israelites. This rules out Muhammad. We have often witnessed how Muslim apologists will only allow for one definition of an English (or Biblical) word when challenging Biblical thinking, especially when Biblical terms have been redefined by Islam in an attempt to make it fit with Islamic theology. The word 'brethren' is one such example.

Also concerning to the Christian mind is the name in which Muhammad spoke. Muhammad did not speak in the Name of the LORD (Yahweh); he spoke in the name of Allah, which, according to the very next verses (Deuteronomy 18:19, 20), makes him a false prophet.

Some Muslims will claim that the 'Helper', of whom Jesus spoke (John 14:16; 17, 26; 15:26; 16:7), is Muhammad, but these texts are clear that it is the Holy Spirit to whom they refer.[67] There is nothing in the Bible that remotely hints at Muhammad. In contrast, Jesus' birth, life, death and resurrection are all prophesied in remarkable detail, meaning that He is the promised Messiah from Heaven. Muhammad's ministry is not authenticated by the Bible.

There is another way to respond to those who claim that Muhammad is prophesied in the Bible. We suggest that you point them to Matthew 24:24, or 2 Peter 2:1-3, both of which discuss false prophets. We are instructed to 'test the spirits' (1 John 4:1-3; in fact, the entire chapter is helpful to share with Muslims).

Summary table of actions performed by Allah, Isa and Muhammad as recorded in the Qur'an

This table shows that even according to the Qur'an, Isa has more attributes in common with Allah than Muhammad does.[68] Yet, Isa still doesn't compare to the divine character and being of Jesus.[69]

Actions	Allah		Isa		Muhammad	
Creates	Q 35:3	✔	Q 3:49	✔		✗
Heals	Q 26:80	✔	Q 5:110	✔	Did no miracles (Q 29:50-51)	✗
Raises the dead	Q 22:6	✔	Q 3:49	✔		✗
Feeds the hungry	Q 6:14	✔	Q 5:112	✔		✗
Changes laws	Q 2:106	✔	Q 3:50	✔	Could not change laws (Q 10:15)	✗
Knows hidden things	Q 5:109	✔	Q 3:49	✔	Only knows what is revealed (Q 6:50)	✗
Knows the last hour	Q 7:187	✔	Q 43:61	✔	Does not know the last hour (Q 72:25)	✗
Is holy/pure/sinless	Q 59:23	✔	Q 19:19	✔	Needs forgiveness (Q 4:106)	✗
Is in heaven	Q 2:255	✔	Q 3:55	✔	Is still in his grave	✗

4

Questions about Muhammad

A note on using Islamic sources

Be careful to only use the earliest Islamic biographies and not recent ones written by modern-day Islamic apologists. These new versions, including those from many of our academic institutions, provide abridged and sanitised versions of the story of Islam, its emergence, and Muhammad's treatment of 'unbelievers'.

'By what authority does Muhammad speak?'

Is it by the authority of the Qur'an?

> Nor does he speak from (his own) inclination. It is not but a revelation revealed (Q 53:3-4 Sahih International).

> There has certainly been for you in the Messenger of Allah an excellent pattern for anyone whose hope is in Allah and the Last Day and [who] remembers Allah often
> (Q 33:21 Sahih International).

> And indeed, you are of a great moral character
> (Q 68:4 Sahih International).

According to Islamic tradition, the stories of the Qur'an came through Muhammad, who was at times alone with a spirit-being in a cave. Muhammad was initially uncertain as to whom he was talking with. After some confusion, and a strange test from his first wife, Khadijah, he agreed with her that it was 'Gabriel'.[70] Although how would she know? She was not with him in the cave.

Who did Muhammad meet? Why would anyone follow a man who was not sure with whom he had spoken? 2 Corinthians 11:14 warns us that 'for Satan himself masquerades as an angel of light'. His words may even tempt human beings to follow him – Jesus stood against this temptation (Matthew 4:1-11), but people can easily be deceived. So, who *did* Muhammad meet?

To say that the Qur'an gives Muhammad authority is not convincing to most non-Muslims, because, according to Islamic tradition, he received the Qur'an himself, alone at the beginning, which means he was a mere man affirming his own authority.

'Why does the Qur'an put Muhammad on a level with Allah?'

O you who believe! Obey Allah, and obey the Messenger... (Q 47:33 Muhsin Khan).

O you who have believed! Obey Allah and His Messenger, and do not turn from him while you hear [his order] (Q 8:20 Sahih International).

The Qur'an challenges its readers to obey Muhammad as they obey Allah. Muslims believe Allah is god, which means Muhammad has been put on a level with god if he is to be obeyed alongside. Surely it is a sin to equate a mere human being, even if he actually were a prophet, with God?

'How do you know that Muhammad is from the true God?'

Did God speak directly to Muhammad or just via an angel (Gabriel)? How do we know that it was the angel Gabriel and not some other spirit? Why was Muhammad confused about whether he was seeing an angel or Satan?[71] Did any of the Biblical prophets believe they were talking to Satan when they were talking to an angel? When the Biblical prophets talked with 'the Angel of the Lord' – Jesus Himself – did they realise they were talking with God? The answer to this last question is 'Yes'. Initially, some may have thought it was an angel, but by the end of the experience they always knew they had seen God (Genesis 16:10-13, 18:1, 22:11-14, 31:11, 32:30, 48:15-16; Exodus 3) and "For I have seen God face to face, and my life is preserved" (Genesis 32:30). At no stage did they wonder whether they had seen a devil, or Satan.

To the Christian, Muhammad's confusion over the identity of the one with whom he was speaking is suspect. More troubling is how Muhammad, the main prophet of Islam, never met the Lord Jesus, never knew His personal name and never talked with Him directly, which means that Muhammad was a 'prophet' (according to Muslim belief) with no direct relationship with God. How can this be?

'Does Muhammad speak by the authority of the Bible?'

Hebrews 1:1-3 shows us that Jesus is the ultimate revelation of God. What does the Bible say of people like Muhammad? Did Muhammad know God's name? Deuteronomy 18:20-22 helps us know whether a prophet is true or false:

> But the prophet who presumes to speak a word in My Name, which I have not commanded him to speak, or who speaks in the name of other gods, that prophet shall die. And if you say in your heart, 'How shall we know the word which the LORD has not spoken?'—When a prophet speaks in the name of the LORD, if the thing does not happen or come to pass, that is the thing which the LORD has not spoken; the prophet has spoken it presumptuously; you shall not be afraid of him.

'If Muhammad is just a man, then why is it blasphemy to speak against him?'

According to the Hadith and Islamic law (the Shariah),[72] insulting Muhammad is a capital offence.[73] The Qur'an tells us that to annoy (some translations say 'abuse') Muhammad brings curses. In Islamic-influenced countries a person can be charged with blasphemy for insulting Muhammad.[74] But Muhammad is not God, so why is criticism of him regarded as blasphemy?

> Those who annoy Allah and His messenger, Allah has cursed them in this world and in the hereafter, and has prepared for them a humiliating punishment (Q 33:57 Yusuf Ali).[75]

> Allah's Messenger said, 'Who will kill Ka'b bin Al-Ashraf who has hurt Allah and His Messenger?' Thereupon Muhammad bin Maslama got up saying, 'O Allah's Messenger! Would you like that I kill him?' The Prophet said, 'Yes' (Bukhari, 5:59:369).

Does this mean that according to Islam, Muhammad is equivalent to Allah in importance?

'If Muhammad is just a man, why does the Qur'an say we have to obey him alongside Allah?'

The Qur'an commands believers to obey Muhammad alongside Allah.

> He who obeys the messenger [Muhammad] has obeyed Allah ... (Q 4:80 Sahih International).

> Oh you who have believed, Obey Allah, and obey the messenger; (Q 47:33 Sahih International).

Isn't this equating Muhammad (a man) with Allah – the greatest of sins in Islam?[76]

'Why did Muhammad have so many wives?'

The Qur'an gave special dispensation to Muhammad, allowing him to have more than the four wives permitted to other Muslim men (Q 4:3, 24), in addition to "those your right hand possesses", which means captives (often taken during warfare), or concubines.[77]

> O Prophet! Lo! We have made lawful unto thee thy wives unto whom thou hast paid their dowries, and those whom thy right hand possesseth of those whom Allah hath given thee as spoils of war, and the daughters of thine uncle on the father's side and the daughters of thine aunts on the father's side, and the daughters of thine uncle on the mother's side and the daughters of thine aunts on the mother's side who emigrated with thee, and a believing woman if she give herself unto the Prophet and the Prophet desire to ask her in marriage – a privilege for thee only, not for the (rest of) believers – We are aware of that which We enjoined upon them concerning their wives and those whom their right hands possess – that thou mayst be free from blame, for Allah is ever Forgiving, Merciful ... (Q 33:50 Pickthall).[78]

Bukhari narrates that Muhammad used to visit all nine or eleven of his wives in one night, depending on the occasion.[79] Al Tabari (regarded by Muslims as an authoritative 10th century Islamic historian) reports that Muhammad "married fifteen women and consummated his marriage with thirteen. He combined eleven at a time and left behind nine."[80] This does not include concubines or sex slaves.

Was this a good example for him to set? Do you want this for your children, especially for your daughters? Why did Muhammad not have to abide by the instructions he gave for all other men?

'Why did Muhammad marry a 6-year-old girl and consummate the marriage when she was 9?'

Bukhari reports that Aisha was six years old when Muhammad married her, and that the marriage was consummated when she was nine years old and Muhammad was around fifty three years old.[81]

Is this a model for today?[82] How does this show good character (Q 68:4) and a model to follow (Q 33:21)?

'Why did Allah break up a marriage for Muhammad?'

According to the Qur'an, Muhammad married his adopted son's wife.

> And [remember, O Muhammad], when you said to the one on whom Allah bestowed favour and you bestowed favour, 'Keep your wife and fear Allah,' while you concealed within yourself that which Allah is to disclose. And you feared the people, while Allah has more right that you fear Him. So, when Zayd had no longer any need for her, We married her to you in order that there not be upon the believers any discomfort concerning the wives of their adopted sons when they no longer have need of them. And ever is the command of Allah accomplished (Q 33:37 Sahih International).

The point is that Muhammad concealed what Allah would do, which was to enable Muhammad to marry Zayd's wife. Does this mean that Muhammad desired her while she was still married to his adopted son, and that Allah arranged for Zayd to divorce her so that Muhammad could marry her? Doesn't this seem like a convenient revelation for Muhammad to say that Allah has provided him a way to marry Zayd's wife? The traditional, authoritative Islamic commentators make it clear that Muhammad lusted after his son's wife.[83] Modern commentators may try to reinterpret this, or even reject some of the traditions of Islam.

Is this the kind of moral example to expect from a 'holy' prophet? What does this say of Allah's character, and his[84] view of marriage and wives?

Muslim friends may respond by pointing to the sinful behaviour of Old Testament prophets and kings. However, the Bible does not hide or condone the sins of our prophets. It presents an honest record of what occurred in history without explaining it away, thereby giving us examples of what *not* to do. The Bible is not a book of dos and don'ts. It is about reality. We learn about God's interaction with His creation, His work in history, now and in the future, and how we can know Him, individually and collectively.

Muhammad's sins, however, are overlooked by Muslims today and are not regarded as sinful. Jesus, by contrast, was and is a pure and a sinless moral example to all creation. Yet, rather than have His Father make things easy for Him (in contrast to Muhammad – Q 33:50: 'in order that there will be upon you no discomfort' [translated "sin" – Pickthall]), Jesus faced the agonies of life, including the burden of our sin, to rescue us from that sin (Psalm 22; Isaiah 53; Hebrews 4:14-15; 1 Peter 3:18).

Our imperfection put the perfect Being on a cross for one reason – to rescue us from God's wrath.

Convenient revelations like that of Q 33:50 are not seen anywhere in the Bible. 'Sinful' lifestyles are recorded in the Bible as accurate reports of history and human behaviour, and presented so that we do not fall into similar behaviour that ultimately harms us (1 Corinthians 10:6,11).

The Lord God has given the world the clearest visual image of how seriously He takes evil. Consider the loving Lord Jesus who, in His darkest hour, just before He was to take on and experience sin for the first time in His eternal life, asked if there was another way (Philippians 2:5-11) – the 'cup' being a symbol of the Lord Jesus' divinely determined destiny (Mark 14:32-36). He asked

His Father if there could be a way not to experience the naked humiliation of physical, emotional, and spiritual agony, which He would shortly endure. Psalm 22 prophesies the agonies that Jesus would endure, as people accused, mocked and hounded Him while He hung, nailed and vulnerable on a tree. The Eternal Son chose what His Father knew must happen – punishment by agonising death in the place of the eternal punishment we would have to suffer (Isaiah 53) because of our failure to live in God's holiness (Romans 3:9-18).

'Why wasn't Muhammad from God's chosen line of prophets?'

The Bible clearly states that God's covenant would be established with the line of Isaac – not Ishmael (Genesis 17:21). Remarkably, the Qur'an agrees with this chosen line for other prophets:

> And We [Allah] gave to Him Isaac and Jacob and placed in
> his descendants prophethood and scripture ...
> (Q 29:27 Sahih International).

That means the prophets would be descended from Isaac and Jacob, as indeed were all the prophets in the Bible. But Muhammad is traditionally believed by Muslims to be a descendant of Ishmael. This means he is not from the chosen prophetic line. What is more, if Muslims wish to claim Ishmael as their 'father', they need to claim the promises about him: 'His hand shall be against every man, and every man's hand against him. And [thus] he shall dwell in the presence of all his brethren' (Genesis 16:12).[85]

Muslims will point out that Ishmael is blessed in the Bible. This opens the door to a good discussion on the difference between Ishmael and Isaac – Ishmael, of human choice, blessed yet in conflict, and not chosen by God to be in the line that will bless the world; Isaac, the promised one, in the genealogy of Jesus, the Son of God (Genesis 22:2; Galatians 3:26-29; Galatians 4:21-31).

It is helpful to tell our Muslim friends that we can only belong to Abraham, regardless of origin, Jew or Gentile, through the Lord Jesus. We, with the believers of old, are saved through belief in God's Son, the Living Lord Jesus! Muslims are mistaken when they think that Jesus was not known to the Old Testament saints (Hebrews 11:24-26).

The letter to the Hebrews is a superb commentary on the Old Testament. It quotes many Old Testament verses, and reflects the deep theology of God, life, human beings, sin, salvation and eternity. It reflects on the One who parallels Moses, yet is 'of more glory than Moses' (Hebrews 3:1-6).

These verses are particularly helpful to point Muslims to, because they believe that Muhammad is the one who parallels Moses. In contrast, the Bible calls us to remember the rebellion of the people against God, as recorded in Exodus, so that we do not do the same. It tells us of the High Priest who has given us the ability to approach God's throne with confidence (Hebrews 4:14-16) – something Muhammad never taught.[86]

Hebrews 11 is a delight to read as we discover how the people of old – not only prophets, and including a repentant prostitute – believed God and acted on their beliefs. They understood who the Lord was and trusted in His promises.

By faith [trust] *Moses ... refused to be called the son of Pharaoh's daughter, choosing rather to suffer affliction with the people of God than to enjoy the passing pleasures of sin, esteeming the reproach of Christ greater riches than the treasures in Egypt ...for he endured as seeing Him who is invisible* (Hebrews 11:24-27; cf. Numbers 12:8).

'Why did Muhammad kill so many people in Medina?'

In the case of the Banu Qurayza tribe, the tribesmen surrendered without a fight, and Muhammad had over 600 of them beheaded.[87] One Hadith narrates:

"I was among the captives of Banu Qurayzah. They (the Companions) examined us, and those who had begun to grow hair (pubes) were killed, and those who had not were not killed. I was among those who had not grown hair." (Abu-Dawud, Book 39, Hadith 4390).[88]

This means that many boys, some as young as twelve, would have been beheaded by Muhammad.[89] This was not done because the boys had engaged in cruelty or heinous evil against others. Whatever your opinion on the death penalty, most people will recognise that evil movements such as ISIS, Al-Shabaab, Boko Haram and Hitler's Nazism sometimes require resisting by military intervention. Muhammad's actions, however, were not a response to evil done to others. His actions were not in obedience to a God who stands up to injustices. In the stories of Muhammad's wars – the biographies known as *the maghazi* [90] (raids) – his battles were for territory, power, wealth, women and captives. Where the Qur'an and the biographical books on his raids reveal a religious reason for them, it is clear that the reason Muhammad fought was that he and Allah were not politically received. A perusal of Islamic history[91] shows that spiritual rescue was not at the heart of his actions but rather, political dominance and the imposition of Islam.[92]

> Indeed, the penalty of those who wage war against Allah and his messenger and strive upon earth [to cause] corruption is none but that they be killed or crucified or that their hands and feet be cut off from opposite sides or that they be exiled from the land. That is for them a disgrace in this world; and for them in the Hereafter a great punishment (Q 5:33 Sahih International).[93]

This verse comes after a verse addressed to the Jews who were given a different approach: 'If you take the life of one, it is as if you take the life of another' (Q 5:32). In these verses the author(s) of the Qur'an seem to recognise that there was a different way that the Bible calls its people to live.

'If Muhammad is the greatest example, why does he seem so unwelcoming?'

Muhammad is clearly held as the example to follow:

> And verily, you are on an exalted standard of character (Q 68:4 Muhsin Khan).

> Indeed in the Messenger of Allah you have a good example to follow for him who hopes in Allah and the Last Day and remembers Allah much (Q 33:21 Muhsin Khan).

The following passage however, shows that Muhammad is not very welcoming:

> O you who believe! Enter not the Prophet's houses, except when leave is given to you for a meal, (and then) not (so early as) to wait for its preparation. But when you are invited, enter, and when you have taken your meal, disperse, without sitting for a talk. Verily, such (behaviour) annoys the Prophet, and he is shy of (asking) you (to go), but Allah is not shy of (telling you) the truth. And when you ask (his wives) for anything you want, ask them from behind a screen; that is purer for your hearts and for their hearts. And it is not (right) for you that you should annoy Allah's Messenger, nor that you should ever marry his wives after him (his death). Verily! With Allah that shall be an enormity (Q 33:53 Muhsin Khan).

This is quite troubling to the Christian mind. As we follow the Lord Jesus, we see that He gave up His throne in Heaven for a life on earth with no place to lay his head (Matthew 8:19-29; Luke 9:57-58), selflessly serving humanity (John 13:1-17).

5

Questions about the Qur'an

When dealing with the Qur'an one needs to take into consideration that, for Muslims, not only the Qur'an, but any element of Islamic content regarding Muhammad, the Caliphs, the Kaaba, etc. are considered to be sacred, and that no criticism, constructive or otherwise, is allowed. They believe that the Qur'an "came down" from the "Eternal Tablet" and therefore, the slightest mistreatment can enrage them. While in the West, we can think of it as just another book, to the Muslim mind it is sacrosanct. As such, Muslims don't write notes in it, tear pages out of it or mishandle it, and they are also required to be ceremonially clean before reading or touching it (Q 56:79).

In countries such as Pakistan, the desecration of the Qur'an carries the death sentence. So, in discussing or critiquing the Qur'an, or other aspects of Islam with a Muslim, there can be strong emotional reactions, as you may be accused of insulting Islam or even discriminating against Muslims and being Islamaphobic. Should any of these allegations be made, you can gently point out to your friend that you respect him or her greatly, and that you are not critiquing their sacred book for the sake of it. On the contrary, the legitimacy and the benchmark for such critique is set by the Qur'an itself, as seen here:

> Do they not, then, ponder about the Qur'ān? Had it been from someone other than Allah, they would have found in it a great deal of discrepancy (Q 4:82 Mufti Taqi Usmani).

These discrepancies can be either internal or external – external referring to the written and unwritten history, to the locations and the variations, and to the absence of any proper narration of Biblical stories, while internal refers to contradictory verses, other inconsistencies, and the doctrine of abrogation in its various forms. It is in order to investigate these apparent discrepancies that we ask questions about the Qur'an.

'Have you read the Qur'an in your own language?'
Few Muslims have actually read what the Qur'an says in a language they understand. They may have learnt to recite some of it in Arabic, without any actual understanding. Your questioning may encourage them to read it with understanding, which is no bad thing once they realise what it says. Be familiar with the Qur'an (a skim read of the first nine chapters will give you an idea of how the book reads). Chapters 4 and 9 make for particularly interesting reading. Chapter 9 is Muhammad's last sermon, according to Islamic tradition. Compare key themes (i.e. God, human beings, sin, salvation and eternity) between the Bible and the Qur'an.

'Why do you say the Qur'an should only be read in Arabic when the Bible can be read in any language?'
Many Muslims will say that the Qur'an should only be read in Arabic. Whilst the Qur'an is translated into many languages, Arabic is still seen as the superior language – the language of Allah. The Bible, however, is translated into hundreds of languages and is readily understood in all of them. What is more, God has, throughout history, met and communicated with people in their respective languages, and continues to do so. We know He created languages from the account of the Tower of Babel (Genesis 11:9). The Lord came down and saw the pride of human beings who believed that they could make their own name supreme. He then scattered the people with multiple new languages. Today, notwithstanding the reason for our numerous languages, He communicates with us in ways we understand.

The Bible is a universal revelation to all people, and we can see this throughout both the Old and New Testaments.

Islamic ritual prayers must be carried out in Arabic in the direction of Arabia. The pilgrimage is to Arabia. The key themes are still called by their Arabic names. The name of Islam's god is a generic Arabic name. We need to ask if Allah can only speak one language. Why is Arabic put on a higher level than all other languages? Why would Allah choose such a new language to be his language? What language did Allah use before Arabic was developed?[94]

Hebrews 11 shows how Jews and converts to Judaism from all nations can be included in Abraham's family – the family of promise. Rahab, the Canaanite, is included in the people of faith alongside Moses. There were many Egyptians who left Egypt in faith, following the Lord into the desert along with the Hebrew slaves (Exodus 12:38). There were God-fearers from many nations who trusted the Lord on the day of Pentecost (Acts 2:5,11).

'Why does the Qur'an have random stories that don't always have a beginning or end or meaning?'
The Bible starts and ends with clearly laid out reports of events and teaching from history. Yet the Qur'an has a very muddled view of history, and certainly not a chronological view. For example, Q 2:247-2:260 presents a convoluted reference to people of history. It starts with Saul, David and Goliath, then moves forward to Isa, son of Mary, and then back to Abraham, followed by a man who was dead for a hundred years and was then raised, and then back to Abraham, all the while weaving warnings throughout the narrative.

You will notice the lack of chronology in the Qur'anic list of the prophets below – quite different from the genealogies in the Old and New Testaments (Genesis 5; Matthew 1:1-17). Included in Islam's list of prophets are Biblical priests (Aaron) and kings (Solomon and David), and also Ishmael, who is not a Biblical prophet:

> Indeed, We have revealed to you, [O Muhammad], as We revealed to Noah and the prophets after him. And we revealed to Abraham, Ishmael, Isaac, Jacob, the Descendants, Jesus, Job, Jonah, Aaron, and Solomon, and to David We gave the book [of Psalms] (Q 4:163 Sahih International).

Nowhere in the Qur'an is there a complete story about a Biblical character. Sura 12, about Joseph, is the closest, and the story of Moses at the burning bush (Q 20:9-36) is close to the account in Exodus 3, except that it excludes one of the most important points of the Biblical story by replacing Yahweh [the Great I AM][95] with Allah. No story in the Qur'an correctly follows the Biblical narrative.

71

We need to ask our Muslim friends why the Qur'an leaves out the most important themes of the Bible. Why does it remove God's personal name? Why does it not show what the former prophets actually taught? If the Qur'an is supposed to be the final revelation, which followed the previous ones (the Torah, Psalms and Injil), why does it contradict them on so many levels – theologically and historically? Which one is true – the detailed narrative that is closest to the events (i.e. the Bible), or the narrative that comes hundreds of years later, with contradictory and muddled stories?[96]

'What is the actual message of the Qur'an?'

Most Muslims will probably suggest that it is about submission to Allah. They might say it is the way to the afterlife. Whatever the answer, it is always helpful to ask for references. We want to understand what the Qur'an is saying, because it concerns us that our Muslim friends follow a book so different from our own, which teaches an altogether different perspective of God.

Why was the Qur'an given? Does it enable you to communicate with God? How? Does it provide a solution for sin and evil in this world? If so, what is it? Does it provide for justice and mercy for all people? Does it show a clear way to salvation? If so, what are the references? Is salvation an Islamic concept? If so, how different is it from Biblical salvation? How does it tell you to live with unbelievers, or even enemies? Can all of Islamic theology, life and practice be found in the Qur'an? If so, where? If not, why not? What are the core themes of the Qur'an? How can it change my life? Does it show how to walk with God in deep communion and relationship as the Bible does? These questions may require some study with your friend. As Christians, we should look at Islam through a Biblical lens and be ready with answers to questions asked about the Bible.[97]

'Where is the *Shahadah* in the Qur'an?'

The *Shahadah* is the confession of faith and is the first of the five pillars of Islam. It says: 'I bear witness that there is no god but Allah, and Muhammad is the prophet of Allah.' This phrase must be said in Arabic by those converting to Islam, and then repeated in religious life as a statement of faith. Though it is very important in Islam, curiously, it does not occur anywhere in this exact form in the Qur'an.

Most Muslims are not aware that the first reference to the *Shahadah* is on the Dome of the Rock in Jerusalem, dated around 691 AD, which is about sixty years after Muhammad's death.[98] The verses on the Dome, including the *Shahadah,* are not exactly the same as in the Qur'an.[99] This is significant as Muslims believe that the Qur'an is preserved, uncreated and unchanged (Q 85:21-22 – uncreated tablets; Q 10:15 and 18:27 – impossible for man to change even a word).[100] Qur'an 15:9 tells us that Allah is guarding the Qur'an: "We will be its guardian." Should it not then include core elements of the Islamic faith such as the conversion statement?

Perhaps this sounds trivial, but is it trivial if your religion is based on obeying exact rules that might give you access into paradise in the afterlife? A study of Islamic law shows how important it is for Muslims to be exact in how they pray, speak, act and live, if they are to have any hope of entering the Islamic paradise.

'Is the Qur'an, or the *Hadith*, or both, the word of Allah?'

The Qur'an is considered the 'word of Allah' to Muslims, although it is not necessarily described this way in the Qur'an. The Qur'an describes itself as 'honoured' and 'preserved' (Q 85:21-22) and a 'revelation'. The Hadith are collections of sayings of Muhammad, and records of his actions. However, without the Hadith, we would not have the five pillars of Islam. A huge portion of Islamic theology is found in the Hadith and in Islamic law. That leads us to ask whether or not the Hadith are inspired. Muslims will take different views on their authority.[101] There are problems either way because of multiple contradictory Hadith and differing opinions on which Hadith are reliable and which are not. Furthermore, the Hadith were compiled over two hundred years after Muhammad's death, and therefore have questionable reliability. Western scholarship, largely ignored by Muslim scholars, has produced some helpful research on the lack of reliability of the Islamic Hadith, Islamic history and the Qur'an.[102]

'Did you know that the Qur'an testifies to the inspiration of the Bible?'

Numerous passages in the Qur'an testify to the inspiration of the Torah (Law of Moses) and the Injeel (the Gospels). See the following examples:

> Say, [O believers], "We have believed in Allah and what has been revealed to us and what has been revealed to Abraham and Ishmael and Isaac and Jacob and the Descendants and what was given to Moses and Jesus and what was given to the prophets from their Lord. We make no distinction between any of them, and we are Muslims [in submission] to Him." (Q 2:136 Sahih International).

> And We sent, following in their footsteps, Jesus, the son of Mary, confirming that which came before him in the Torah; and We gave him the Gospel, in which was guidance and light and confirming that which preceded it of the Torah as guidance and instruction for the righteous (Q 5:46 Sahih International).

> He has sent down upon you, [O Muhammad], the Book in truth, confirming what was before it. And He revealed the Torah and the Gospel. Before, as guidance for the people. And He revealed the Qur'an. Indeed, those who disbelieve in the verses of Allah will have a severe punishment, and Allah is exalted in Might, the Owner of Retribution (Q 3:3-4 Sahih International).

> Indeed, We have revealed to you, [O Muhammad], as We revealed to Noah and the prophets after him. And we revealed to Abraham, Ishmael, Isaac, Jacob, the Descendants, Jesus, Job, Jonah, Aaron, and Solomon, and to David We gave the book [of Psalms] (Q 4:163 Sahih International).

> And before it was the scripture of Moses to lead and as a mercy. And this is a confirming Book in an Arabic tongue to warn those who have wronged and as good tidings to the doers of good (Q 46:12 Sahih International).

We see here multiple verses from the Qur'an testifying to the inspiration of the Bible.[103] This should surely mean that any serious Muslim would want to read the Bible.[104]

'Why does the Qur'an say Jesus didn't die by crucifixion when historical references to it from the first two centuries say He did?'

The Qur'an clearly denies that Jesus died by crucifixion:

> And [for] their saying, "Indeed, we have killed the Messiah, Jesus, the son of Mary, the messenger of Allah." And they did not kill him, nor did they crucify him; but [another] was made to resemble him to them. And indeed, those who differ over it are in doubt about it. They have no knowledge of it except the following of assumption. And they did not kill him, for certain (Q 4:157 Sahih International).

This contrasts sharply with the testimony of the Gospels, the New Testament, early Christians, and every other early historian who writes about the subject. Non-Christian historians who report that Jesus died by crucifixion include Tacitus (c. AD 100-110), Thallus (c. AD 52), and Josephus (c. AD 93-94).[105]

The Qur'an claims to have been written some six hundred years after Jesus' death. It stretches credulity to believe that Muhammad knew better than the earliest witnesses and reporters. There is no first century historian or writer that denies Jesus' death. Ideas suggesting that Jesus did not die (as is written in the Qur'an), or that there was a division of the divine from the material body, did not emerge till the mid-to-late 2nd century, largely through heretical writing, which the early Church Fathers refuted.[106]

'Why did Muhammad not quote from the Old Testament?'

Because the names of Ibrahim (Abraham), Moses (Musa) and others are mentioned in the Qur'an, many believe that the Qur'an copied its stories from the Bible. However, there is no story that accurately parallels the Biblical accounts. The closest is that of Moses standing before the burning bush. Yet, even here, it misses out the most important aspect of the Biblical account. Exodus 3:14-15 are important verses to share.

The LORD [YHWH, or Yahweh] God of your fathers, the God of Abraham, the God of Isaac [not Ishmael], and the God of Jacob, has sent me to you. This is My name forever ...

This clear presentation of His name – the name that is to be used by all prophets (See Deuteronomy 18:19-20) – is left out of the Qur'anic story. The Qur'an never quotes from the Old Testament nor accurately relates stories from the Old Testament. So, where do the stories in the Qur'an come from?

'Did you know that many Qur'anic stories of characters from the Bible come from heretical literature, Jewish stories or Christian traditions outside the Bible?'
Here are some quotations from respected writers on Islam.

The many errors that occur in the Qur'an show that Muhammad received his information orally, and probably from men who had no great amount of book-learning themselves.[107]

The impression the Kuran[108] makes on the reader is that its Jewish fibre has been spun from hearsay and scraps of information gathered from conversation with different persons.[109]

Qur'anic reference	Theme of story	Likely origin of story
Q 21:62-68	A story of Abraham and idols	Midrash Rabbah (Jewish folklore embellishing Biblical material)
Q 5:30-35	A story of Cain and Abel	This is a compilation of accounts taken from the Targum of Jonathan Ben Uzzziah, the Midrash Rabbah, and Mishnah Sanhedrin, 4.5 (a Jewish commentary on the Torah) – all 1st-2nd centuries[110]
Q 19:27-34	Isa speaks as a baby	Arabic Infancy Gospel (5th-6th centuries)
Q 3:49; Q 5:110	Isa makes clay birds and gives them life	Infancy Gospel of Thomas (2nd century)

Qur'anic reference	Theme of story	Likely origin of story
Q 19:22-26	Qur'anic version of the birth of Isa	Infancy Gospel of Pseudo-Matthew (early 7th century)
Q 18:9-26	Young men who miraculously slept for 300 years	Story of 'the Seven Sleepers' found in Syriac sources (5th-6th centuries)

A comparison of the stories, laid out side by side, may prompt your Muslim friends to doubt the integrity of the Qur'an. This is important if we wish to introduce them to the historically verified Bible. In the words of Nelson Glueck, "no archaeological discovery has ever controverted a properly understood Biblical statement."[111]

Recent research shows that Muhammad probably had nothing to do with the Qur'an, which, according to Islamic tradition, had been compiled by the Caliph Uthman by 652 AD. However, all extant earliest manuscripts are too late to be credible, as they are dated from the mid-to-late 8th century or later. Where is that 652 AD Qur'an? Furthermore, the various versions of the Qur'an should agree with one another if the Islamic claim of a 'preserved, unchanged Qur'an' is to be taken seriously.[112]

For more research on the matter, consider the work of Dr. Ekmeleddin İhsanoğlu[113] and Dr Tayyar Altıkulaç[114] on the Topkapi manuscript (one of the six earliest texts of the Qur'an in existence today):

We have none of Uthman's Mushafs [manuscripts] ...

Nor do we have any of the copies from those Mushafs ...

These Mushafs date from the later 'Umayyad period' ...[115]

There are deviations from grammatical rules (Laḥn) and spelling mistakes in the Muṣḥafs attributed to Caliph 'Uthmān' ...[116]

2,270 instances where there is a difference from the [consonantal skeleton] of the Fahd Muṣḥaf ...[117]

A note on the Islamic Traditions

Understanding exactly what happened in Islamic history is difficult, as many of the early traditions of Islam derive from stories written almost 200 years after the events. None of the traditions of Islam were written down until 833 AD; Muhammad died in 632 AD, according to Islamic tradition. These dates leave historians questioning the reliability of the traditions of Islam.

Biography of Muhammad: Siraby ibn-Hisham (c. 833 AD), Sayings of Muhammad: Hadith by al-Bukhari (c. 870 AD)[118], Histories of Islam: Tarikh written by al-Tabari (c. 923 AD), Commentaries of the Qur'an: Tafsir by a variety of authors, and, among others, al-Baladhuri (c. 892 AD), az-Zamaḥšarî (c. 1144), al-Baydawi (c. 1282 AD), and al-Suyuti (c. 1502 AD).

6

Questions on Women in Islam

'What does the Qur'an say about women?'

You may receive a romanticised response, but rarely would our Muslim friends have read the Qur'an concerning its references to women in their relationship to men. Here follows a list of verses to aid you in your discussions. This is difficult material, so keep in mind that you are highlighting this information because you care for the person who says they follow the Qur'an. If these verses were applied in your life, would they have a negative or positive impact on you and your family?

Q 2:223 – women are a tilth [field] for their husbands to 'go into when and how they wish'[119];

Q 2:230 – reconciliation after divorce can only happen after a woman has consummated a marriage with another man, is then divorced by that man, and then returned to the first husband;

Q 2:282 – a woman's testimony is half that of a man;

Q 4:3 – a man can have a polygamous marriage while women are not permitted to have more than one husband; married women are treated more fairly compared to slave girls;

Q 4:3b – "except what your right hand possesses". This implies that men can have and can treat slave girls as they wish; (Q 4:24-25; 23:6; 24:34; 33:50; 70:30). This 'get-out clause' of exceptions to the rule puts non-Muslim and slave women in a precarious position; it is also a direct disobedience of the 7th of the 10 commandments ("You shall not commit adultery" – Exodus 20:14);

Q 4:11 – women receive only half the inheritance that men receive;

Q 4:15 – lewd wives/women are kept in their houses until death;

Q 4:24 – it is permissible for Muslim men to marry, or pay for contracted sex with married slaves;[120]

Q 4:25 – if a man is poor and lacks self-control, he is permitted to marry slave girls;

Q 4:34a – men excel women;

Q 4:34b – righteous women are devoutly obedient to their husbands;

Q 4:34c – corporal punishment (i.e. beating of wives) is permitted if the husband suspects wrong-doing, or disobedience;

Q 4:129 – the Qur'an admits that men are unable to treat wives equally;

Q 5:6 – men are to purify themselves after going to the toilet, or being in physical contact with a woman; note this is not sexual contact – that is mentioned earlier on in the verse;

Q 33:33 – Muhammad's wives are encouraged to stay in their houses;

Q 33:50 – Muhammad can have women who offer themselves to him – a privilege only for him;

Q 33:51 – Muhammad was initially allowed to set aside or take on any wife he willed;

Q 33:52 – a limit was then introduced concerning how many Muhammad could take, except that which *his right hand possessed* – another example of an exemption clause uniquely reserved for Muhammad;

Q 33:53a – permission was needed to enter Muhammad's house because he was easily annoyed;

Q 33:53 – Allah reveals this verse because Muhammad was too shy to, so Allah said it for him: "Allah wishes no discomfort on Muhammad";

Q 33:53b – Muhammad's wives had to stay behind a screen when a male visited the home;

Q 33:59 – the covering of Muhammad's wives and believing women is so they are not bothered by men;

Q 65:1 – instructions are given on how to divorce wives;

Q 65:4 – a contested and debated verse (in recent times) about whether prepubescent women can be married and divorced;

Q 66:1-2 – Allah gives an edict that Muhammad uniquely can be absolved from his oaths;

Q 66:4-5 – Muhammad's wives are threatened by Allah with divorce if they continue to disobey Muhammad. In this context Muhammad could break his oaths and marriages to his wives if they divulged a secret of his.

'Why are there so few verses in the Qur'an instructing men to be kind to women?'

The Qur'anic verses above do not stand up against the Biblical sacrificial love a husband is to have for his wife (Ephesians 5:25), especially keeping in mind that our model is the eternal love seen between the persons of the Trinity, and Jesus' love for the church – whom He calls His 'bride' (Isaiah 54:5; Revelation 21:9; Ephesians 5:27).

Q 30:21 (Sahih International) says: ' ... He placed between you affection and mercy'. 'Affection' is closer to the meaning in Arabic though modern translations say 'love'. Nevertheless, even though translated as 'love', it is not the sacrificial love of the New Testament (Ephesians 5:25). What does 'affection' and 'mercy' mean in the light of verses on women described as a husband's 'tilth' (a field to be ploughed: Q 2:222-223), and 'beaten' (Q 4:34), easily divorced (Q 2:230; 65:1-6), made the second or third wife (Q 4:3; 33:50), and taken as slaves (Q 4:24; 23:6; 24:34; 33:50; 70:30)? Why would

Allah call for 'affection and mercy' between a husband and wife when he invokes punishment and threat in the rest of his edicts concerning how a man should treat his wife (see Q 65:1-4; 66:1-6)?

What exactly does kindness mean in the Qur'an, since there is no example shown by the god of Islam of the kind of sacrificial love, unity, kindness, respect, submission, longing, delight and eternal relationship seen and experienced by those who know and love Yahweh?

'Why does the Qur'an treat women as lesser citizens?'

The Qur'an has several verses that are clearly discriminatory against women. For example, the following verse states that the testimonies of two women are equal to the testimony of one man:

> ... get two witnesses, out of your own men, and if there are not two men, then a man and two women, such as ye choose, for witnesses, so that if one of them errs, the other can remind her (Q 2:282 Yusuf Ali).

A woman's testimony is therefore worth half that of a man. Men have permission to marry up to four wives, yet women are not able to marry more than one husband (Q 4:3). Women are entitled to half the inheritance of males (Q 4:11). This might have made more sense in 7th century Arabia, but is it applicable today, when many women are living single lives, with no "male guardians"?[121] Women are instructed to be obedient, and permission is given to abuse them (Q 4:34 Yusuf Ali).

'Why does the Qur'an allow women to be abused?'

> As to those women on whose part ye fear disloyalty and ill-conduct, admonish them (first), (next), refuse to share their beds, (And last) beat them (lightly); but if they return to obedience, seek not against them Means (of annoyance) (Q 4:34 Yusuf Ali).[122]

In some of the most recent English Qur'anic translations, often distributed at Muslim book tables for purposes of 'Da'wah' ('to invite' – Islamic mission), the word *id'ribūhunna*, meaning 'strike them', has been removed. However, this is an inaccurate handling of the Arabic text.

Most other English translations better portray the meaning of the Arabic word:

Sahih International: 'strike them'

Pickthall: 'scourge them'

Yusuf Ali: 'beat them' ('lightly' is put in brackets in many translations, but this is not implied by the Arabic word or tense).

The God of the Bible hates abuse of others, and a man is called to sacrifice himself for his wife, just as Christ loved the 'Church' – His 'Bride' – and gave Himself for it (Isaiah 62:5; Ephesians 5:25; Revelation 19:7-9; 22:17).

'Does the Qur'an support sexual-slavery?'

Certainly 'those whom their right hands possess of believing slave girls' in the verse below has traditionally been interpreted by Islamic theologians as female captives used for sex.[123] This means that women can be owned as sex-slaves. Women are taken, or married, usually in the context of a man seeking *nikah* (sex).[124]

And whoever among you cannot [find] the means to marry free, believing women, then [he may marry] from those whom your right hands possess of believing slave girls (Q 4:25 Sahih International).[125]

In the biographies and histories of Muhammad, he traded slave girls. For example, Al Tabari relates that Dihyah had asked the Messenger for Safiyah when the Prophet chose her for himself. The Apostle then traded Safiyah by giving Dihyah her two cousins. The women of Khaybar were distributed among the Muslims.[126]

Juwayriya bint al-Harith was taken as booty by Muhammad after his men killed her husband. She was a Jewess, the very beautiful wife of the chief. When she tried to buy her freedom she caught Muhammad's eye and he married her.[127]

Mariyah al-Quptiya was a beautiful Coptic concubine (possibly sent as a gift from the governor of Egypt). According to Islamic tradition, there was an occasion when Muhammad went to his wife Hafsa, and, on finding that she was out, took her slave girl, Mariyah, instead. Hafsa caught them. The slave girl got pregnant but the baby died.[128]

Muhammad was given freedom by Allah to take female prisoners of war for marriage.

O Prophet, indeed We have made lawful to you your wives to whom you have given their due compensation and those your right hand possesses from what Allah has returned to you [of captives] and the daughters of your paternal uncles and the daughters of your paternal aunts and the daughters of your maternal uncles and the daughters of your maternal aunts who emigrated with you and a believing woman if she gives herself to the Prophet [and] if the Prophet wishes to marry her, [this is] only for you, excluding the [other] believers. We certainly know what We have made obligatory upon them concerning their wives and those their right hands possess, [but this is for you] in order that there will be upon you no discomfort. And ever is Allah Forgiving and Merciful (Q 33:50 Sahih International).

It is well known that a man may divorce a wife simply by uttering the words "I divorce you" three times on three separate occasions, whereas it is much harder for a woman to obtain a divorce (Q 2:229). This verse tells us that if the woman wishes for a divorce, she 'ransoms herself' (Sahih International), 'gives something for her freedom' (Yusuf Ali), or 'pays a ransom to set herself free' (Hilali/Khan).

These aspects of the Qur'an are still applied today by many conservative Muslims. Is this not troubling for your Muslim friends? If the Qur'an is preserved in Heaven, presumably this has been Allah's view of women all along?

In response, Muslims may find stories in the Bible which they think also show mistreatment of women. There *are* stories of women being ill-treated, such as rape victims, but not as an edict or allowance from God. The Bible reports human history and behaviour without concealing faults and mistakes. The Lord God acted firmly against the abuse of women and vulnerable people. Deuteronomy 22:25-27 safeguards women who had been violated, with the perpetrator receiving the death penalty. James 1:27 shows faith in action, which pleases God: 'Pure and undefiled religion before God and the Father is this: to visit orphans and widows in their trouble, and to keep oneself unspotted from the world.'

Consider also Psalm 146:9: 'The Lord watches over the strangers; He relieves the fatherless and widow; But the way of the wicked He turns upside down.' O that Muhammad had followed this verse! If Muhammad is from God, why did he ignore such clear edicts? Wouldn't the lives of women, including the women he widowed, and the concubines he took, have been spared?

'Does Islamic marriage reflect your relationship with Allah?'
Marriage in the Bible is deeply connected to the ultimate marriage – the appearance of the Bridegroom, the Lord Jesus, to marry His bride, the church (Revelation 19:6-9). This might sound strange to those outside the Christian faith. How can God marry us? Jesus obviously enjoyed weddings – one of his first miracles was turning water into wine at a wedding (John 2:1-11). The Lord God describes himself as the 'husband' of his people (Isaiah 54:5; Hosea 2:19; Jeremiah 31:32; Jeremiah 2:1-11), and lets us read about His broken heart when his people desert Him for other 'gods', idols and lesser loves, that ultimately do not satisfy.

Marriage in the Bible is taught in the context of Jesus and His love and commitment to the Church. One husband – one church. Ephesians 5:32 tells how the marriage union is a metaphor for Jesus' union with the church. This is why Islamic marriage is devastating to the Christian, because it allows for the abuse of vulnerable women, with its multiplicity of wives, the ownership of slave women, and the ease of divorce for men. Islam is ignorant of the loving devotion of Jesus Christ, the 'husband' who died for His bride, the church.

For some, this becomes too personal, too uncomfortable to describe the Lord in such terms, but these are *His* terms. And if they are – what does that tell us about God? What does this tell us about His character – that He describes Himself as the husband of the Church? Would Allah ever relate to us with such tenderness, strength and grace? Would Allah ever want to walk with humanity in the deepest of relationships – in a relationship of promise, commitment and safety – a relationship that is secure, steadfast, trustworthy and eternal?

When beliefs, religious or otherwise, take us away from this picture of what God is like, then surely those beliefs result in us missing out on the deepest fulfilment the human heart could long for.

7

Questions on Violence

'Why does the Qur'an advocate so much violence'

There are over one hundred and fifty verses in the Qur'an that prescribe violence for the sake of Islamic rule and belief.[129] These are mostly open-ended, and not constrained to a particular historical context.[130] There are a few verses of tolerance and these are early verses, traditionally believed to be abrogated by the later and more authoritative verses prescribing violence.[131] Here are some examples:

> And when the sacred months have passed, then kill the polytheists wherever you find them and capture them and besiege them and sit in wait for them at every place of ambush. But if they should repent, establish prayer, and give zakah [Islamic obligatory charity donations], let them [go] on their way. Indeed, Allah is Forgiving and Merciful (Q 9:5 Sahih International).

> And kill them wherever you overtake them and expel them from wherever they have expelled you, and fitnah [persecution] is worse than killing. And do not fight them at al-Masjid al-Haram until they fight you there. But if they fight you, then kill them. Such is the recompense of the disbelievers (Q 2:191 Sahih International).

> Indeed, the penalty for those who wage war against Allah and His Messenger and strive upon earth [to cause] corruption is none but that they be killed or crucified or that their hands and feet be cut off from opposite sides or that they be exiled from the land. That is for them a disgrace in this world; and for them in the Hereafter is a great punishment, Except for those who return [repenting] before you apprehend them. And know that Allah is Forgiving and Merciful (Q 5:33-34 Sahih International).

This violence is rarely to take a stand against heinous crime, or great evil (see the next question for reasons for violence in the Qur'an). Muhammad was a person who committed murder, and this type of violent act is frequently commanded in the Qur'an.

'Why does the Qur'an command killing for simply disbelieving Islam?'

Here are two verses that command such killing:

> Fight those who believe not in Allah nor the Last Day, nor hold that forbidden which hath been forbidden by Allah and His Messenger, nor acknowledge the religion of Truth, (even if they are) of the People of the Book, until they pay the Jizya [money paid by non-Muslims living in Muslim lands] with willing submission, and feel themselves subdued (Q 9:29 Yusuf Ali).

> And fight them until there is no fitnah and [until] the religion, all of it, is for Allah ... (Q 8:39 Sahih International).

The crime here is unbelief specifically in Allah, Islamic prayer, almsgiving, Islam's day of judgment, and laws laid out by Muhammad and attributed to Allah. It is given in the context of political submission – not criminal law. Is the death penalty appropriate for unbelief in a specific creed or practice? Is the death penalty justified for not obeying a mere man, even if he is seen by some to be a prophet of a new religion?[132] Surely only God can judge the beliefs of the human heart. Shouldn't judgment only be administered for crimes committed against God and humanity? Ultimately the only one who knows whether or not to administer punishment is the One who sees all things. Did Muhammad see all things? Was he a ruler of nations or a tribal warrior suppressing nations? Was he just?

If the Qur'an follows on from the previous revelation (i.e. the Bible) as it claims, why would it have such unjust and different criteria for the harshest penalty – capital punishment?[133]

'Why does Islam teach the death penalty for apostasy?'

Death for apostasy is taught in the Qur'an (Q 4:89, 9:73), and even more explicitly in the Hadith, where Muhammad is reported as saying:

> If somebody (a Muslim) discards his religion, kill him (Bukhari, 4:52:260).

And again:

> Whoever changed his Islamic religion, then kill him (Bukhari, 9:84:57).

The classic manual of Shafi'i Islamic jurisprudence, *The Reliance of the Traveller*, affirms:

> When a person who has reached puberty and is sane voluntarily apostatises from Islam, he deserves to be killed (*Reliance of the Traveller*, O8.1, p. 595).[134]

In fact, all four schools of Sunni Islamic jurisprudence agree on the death penalty for apostasy, as do Shi'ite schools of law. Why is there no freedom of religion under Islam? Should people be killed just because they choose to leave Islam?

'How do you feel about Muhammad imposing severe punishments on sinners?'

The Christian understands the severity of punishment sin requires, but the key difference is the cross of Christ. The price has been paid. Mohammad, meanwhile, meted out punishments while he himself was exempted from them. To ask a question on this topic you would need to have some references. A few will suffice. Here are a couple of examples which are helpful to point out:[135]

About thieves:

The Qur'an is a Muslim's highest authority, with content that closely mirrors Muhammad's life and actions. Consider the following verses from the Qur'an and the Hadith:

[As for] the thief, the male and the female, amputate their hands in recompense for what they committed as a deterrent [punishment] from Allah . And Allah is Exalted in Might and Wise (Q 5:38 Sahih International).

...the penalty for those who wage war against Allah and His Messenger and strive upon earth [to cause] corruption is none but that they be killed or crucified or that their hands and feet be cut off from opposite sides or that they be exiled from the land (Q 5:33a Sahih International).

Narrated Abu Huraira: Allah's Apostle said, 'Allah curses the thief who steals an egg (or a helmet) for which his hand is to be cut off, or steals a rope, for which his hand is to be cut off' (Bukhari V8 Bk81 h791).[136]

About drunk people:

Narrated Ansa bin Malik: 'The Prophet beat a drunk with palm-leaf stalks and shoes. And Abu Bakr gave (such a sinner) forty lashes' (Bukhari V8 Bk81 h764).[137]

Against enemies of Muhammad and Islam:

The prophet ordered for some iron pieces to be made red hot, and their eyes were branded with them and their hands and feet were cut off and were not cauterized... when they asked for water they were not given till they died (Bukhari V8 Bk82 h796,[138] Q 5:33)

About fighting:

[Shafi'i] taught Allah has imposed the duty of 'jihad as laid down in His Book and uttered by Prophet's tongue'. He stressed the calling of men to fulfil the jihad based on Qur'anic edicts, such as Q 9:3, 36, 5, 29 (*Shafi'i*, Al-Risala, Chapter 3, p. 83).

Many Muslims are peaceful and would not hurt anyone physically. They are shocked when these examples from the Qur'an and

Muhammad's life are pointed out to them. This is why it is so important to help people understand that we judge our religions, not according to someone's opinions, but according to 'the book and the man'. Once these particular verses and traditions are referenced – and there are many in the Qur'an, the Hadith, biography (Sira), and Islamic law – introduce your Muslim friend to the only alternative, which is the life and teaching of Lord Jesus Christ.

We also advise you to read around these issues further, because of the varied views Muslims have regarding which traditions are authoritative and which are not. A complex 'science of oral tradition' hinders many lay Muslims from understanding Islamic texts for themselves. Questions on the verses we present here are still helpful, but be ready for a variety of responses such as: "These are not applicable today." or "This is not a reliable Hadith." or "I only follow the Qur'an…" For the liberal Muslim, this last comment may well be true. For many of our friends the only way to cope with some of the brutal verses in their traditions is to pick and choose which ones to follow.

'Why are there so many direct commands encouraging violence towards unbelievers in the Qur'an?'

Table of references to violence encouraged in the Qur'an

2:178	2:179	2:190	2:191	2:193	2:194	2:216	2:217	2:218	2:244
3:121	3:122	3:123	3:124	3:125	3:126	3:140	3:141	3:146	3:152
3:153	3:154	3:155	3:156	3:157	3:165	3:166	3:167	3:169	3:172
3:173	3:195	4:71	4:72	4:74	4:75	4:76	4:77	4:84	4:89
4:90	4:91	4:94	4:095	4:100	4:102	4:104	5:33	5:35	5:82
8:1	8:5	8:7	8:9	8:12	8:15	8:16	8:17	8:39	8:40
8:41	8:42	8:43	8:44	8:45	8:46	8:47	8:48	8:57	8:58
8:59	8:60	8:65	8:66	8:67	8:68	8:69	8:70	8:71	8:72
8:73	8:74	8:75	9:5	9:12	9:13	9:14	9:16	9:19	9:20
9:24	9:25	9:26	9:29	9:36	9:38	9:39	9:41	9:44	9:52
9:73	9:81	9:83	9:86	9:88	9:92	9:111	9:120	9:122	9:123
16:110	22:39	22:58	22:78	24:53	24:55	25:52	29:6	29:69	33:15
33:18	33:20	33:25	33:26	33:27	33:50	47:4	47:20	48:15	48:16
48:17	48:22	48:24	49:15	59:2	59:5	59:6	59:7	59:8	59:14
60:9	61:4	61:11	61:13	63:4	64:14	66:9	73:20	76:8	

Here are extracts from some of the relevant verses:[139]

So let those fight in the cause of Allah who sell the life of this world for the Hereafter. And he who fights in the cause of Allah, and is killed or achieves victory, We shall bestow on him a great reward (Q 4:74 Sahih International).

So do not take from among them [those whom Allah sends astray – Q 4:88] allies until they emigrate for the cause of Allah. But if they turn away, then seize them and kill them wherever you find them and take not from among them any ally or helper (Q 4:89 Sahih International).

[Remember] when your Lord inspired to the angels, "I am with you, so strengthen those who have believed. I will cast terror into the hearts of those who disbelieved, so strike [them] upon the necks and strike from them every fingertip" (Q 8:12 Sahih International).

And fight them until there is no fitnah and [until] the religion, all of it, is for Allah. And if they cease – then indeed, Allah is Seeing of what they do (Q 8:39 Sahih International).

And prepare against them whatever you are able of power and of steeds of war by which you may terrify the enemy of Allah and your enemy and others besides them whom you do not know [but] whom Allah knows. And whatever you spend in the cause of Allah will be fully repaid to you, and you will not be wronged (Q 8:60 Sahih International).

And when the sacred months have passed, then kill the polytheists ['Musrikun' translated as 'pagans' 'idolaters' 'polytheists' 'unbelievers'] wherever you find them and capture them and besiege them and sit in wait for them at every place of ambush. But if they should repent, establish prayer, and give zakah, let them [go] on their way. Indeed, Allah is Forgiving and Merciful (Q 9:5 Sahih International).

So when you meet those who disbelieve [in battle], strike [their] necks until, when you have inflicted slaughter upon them, then secure their bonds, and either [confer] favor afterwards or ransom [them] until the war lays down its burdens... (Q 47:4 Sahih International).

Some Muslims will say that there is a context in which to understand these verses. The difficulty is that the Qur'an itself rarely provides any context. Contexts are given by Islamic thinkers some 200 or more years later.[140]

Be sensitive to your Muslim friends as you introduce them to Islamic traditions and Qur'anic verses that they are likely to find shocking. Take for example, 'I will cast terror into the hearts of those who disbelieved, so strike [them] upon the necks and strike from them every fingertip' (Q 8:12 Sahih International). We must not shy away from tackling tough topics, but we need to be aware that we will be dealing with material that could trigger emotional responses. These are issues that strike at the heart of people's beliefs and can be quite shocking for the average Muslim who has never read the Qur'an.

'Is Islam a religion of peace?'

It is widely repeated that Islam is a 'religion of peace'. However, when we come face to face with instructions in the Qur'an urging violence, and examples set by Muhammad, this view becomes hard to sustain.

This question is not about whether Muslims are generally peaceful people. Very often they are. What we need to do is determine whether a religion is a 'religion of peace' according to its teaching and the example set by its founder.

The word 'Islam' does not mean 'peace' as is often assumed. It means 'submission' or 'surrender'. In its original meaning, a Muslim was someone who had surrendered in warfare.[141] Islam was first called a 'religion of peace' only as recently as 1930, in a book published to promote Islam.[142] The expression did not appear in Islamic history up to then.

As we have seen in this section, the teachings of the Qur'an and the example set by Muhammad do not promote peace. Islam should not therefore be described as a 'religion of peace'.

One verse that is sometimes cited to argue that the Qur'an does not promote violence is Q 5:32. It is quoted like this:

... if anyone killed a person, it would be as if he killed all mankind; and if anyone saved a life, it would be as if he saved the life of all mankind.

This may be the most misquoted verse in the Qur'an. The whole verse provides the context:

On that account: We ordained for the Children of Israel *'Children of men' [emphasis ours]* that if any one slew a person – unless it be for murder or for spreading mischief in the land – it would be as if he slew the whole people: and if any one saved a life, it would be as if he saved the life of the whole people. Then although there came to them Our messengers with clear signs, yet, even after that, many of them continued to commit excesses in the land (Q 5:32 Yusuf Ali).

Notice that this command is described as having been ordained for 'the Children of Israel', that is, Jewish people. It is not said to be a command for Muslims today. Even if it were ordained for Muslims today, there is an exception clause that is conveniently left out of the quotation: '...unless it be for murder or for spreading mischief in the land'. The question then arises as to what constitutes 'mischief' (*fasadin*). The term is very broad. In one passage in the Qur'an, merely disputing Islam is regarded as making mischief (Q 3:60-63). In another passage, rejecting Allah is making mischief (Q 7:103). There is a Hadith that explains that this passage refers to polytheists (Sunan Abu Dawud 38:4359). The classical commentary on the Qur'an, Tafsir Ibn Kathir (2:11), explains:

'Do not make mischief on the earth', means 'Do not commit acts of disobedience on the earth'. Their mischief is disobeying Allah, because whoever disobeys Allah on the earth, or commands that Allah be disobeyed, he has committed mischief on the earth.[143]

So, 'making mischief' can be seen as any form of disobedience to Allah. This would make any non-Muslim or disobedient Muslim an exception to the instruction not to kill a person.

The very next verse of the Qur'an then goes on to clarify, this time not only for Jews but for Muslims also, what should be done to those who spread mischief through the land:

> The punishment of those who wage war against Allah and His Messenger, and strive with might and main for mischief through the land is: execution, or crucifixion, or the cutting off of hands and feet from opposite sides, or exile from the land: that is their disgrace in this world, and a heavy punishment is theirs in the Hereafter (Q 5:33 Yusuf Ali).

The above verse encourages Muslims to kill or maim those who spread mischief in the land, which, as we have seen, could also refer to any non-Muslim.

Jesus, in contrast, taught us to love our enemies and to pray for those who persecute us (Matthew 5:44). There are no parallel commands anywhere in the Qur'an. It is Christianity that is deserving of the description 'religion of peace', whereas Islam is not.[144]

'Is Islamic law kind to unbelievers?'

There are four schools of law in Sunni (majority) Islam: Hanafi, Hanbali, Maliki and Al-Shafi. Shi'a Muslims would follow some of these and other schools of laws. They would usually consider Al-Jafri to be the authoritative source.

When to desist fighting unbelievers in war:

> Fighting unbelievers is obligatory, even if they do not initiate it against us ... When Muslims enter territory at war [with the Muslims] (dar al-harb) and they lay siege to a city or to a fort, they invite [the inhabitants] to Islam. If [the inhabitants] accept them, [then] [the Muslims] desist from fighting them, but if they decline [the Muslims] call them to pay Jizyah. If they give it (Jizyah), then they have [as a legal right] whatever the Muslims have, and [the legal

duties] due on them are whatever are due on [the Muslims]
... (Al-Quduri, Hanafi School, pp. 661-662).[145]

On unbelievers paying the *Jizyah* (subjugation tax):

They should be in a state of humility when it is taken from
them ... It is not taken from them in a gentle or pleasant
manner. Instead it is taken from them in a manner that
rebukes them for having disbelieved in Allah for belying the
Messenger of Allah. If these conditions are met, the jizya is
accepted from them ... (Hanbali, pp. 765-766).[146]

On the second-class citizenship of unbelievers (Dhimmi status):

The Dhimmis are treated according to Islamic law by
the imam with regards to life, wealth, and honour and al-
hudud [death penalty] is imposed upon them in that which
they consider forbidden, not in that which they consider
permissible ... (Hanbali, p. 768).

Dhimmis are to be clearly distinguished from Muslims.
They cannot ride a horse. Nor can they have centre stage at
events. They are not to be greeted with peace. Dhimmis are
forbidden to build churches. Their houses cannot be taller
than Muslim homes. Their religion must be hidden away,
and not made public (Hanbali, pp. 770-771).

It is important to note that Islamic law is complex and has
multiple variations throughout its texts. As in the Hadith and
Tarikh (histories of Islam), variations of stories and examples are
presented. That said, regardless of these variations, there are many
challenging statements within Islamic law towards unbelievers,
women, slaves and apostates.

8

Miscellaneous Questions: Abrogation and Satanic Verses

'Why does the Qur'an have abrogation?'

Islam teaches the concept of abrogation, meaning later verses 'abrogate' or 'cancel' earlier verses. This means that Muhammad, and presumably Allah (if the text is believed to have come from Allah on preserved tablets – see Q 85:22), were able to override earlier revelations with later ones. This concept of abrogation is used to explain apparently contradictory instructions in the Qur'an. While some modern Muslims may wish to reject the law of abrogation, abrogation is taught in the Qur'an:

> We do not abrogate a verse or cause it to be forgotten except that We bring forth [one] better than it or similar to it. Do you not know that Allah is over all things competent? (Q 2:106 Sahih International).

> Allah doth blot out or confirm what He pleaseth: with Him is the Mother of the Book (Q 13:39 Yusuf Ali).

> If it were Our Will, We could take away that which We have sent thee by inspiration: then wouldst thou find none to plead thy affair in that matter as against Us (Q 17:86 Yusuf Ali).

> And when We substitute a verse in place of a verse – and Allah is most knowing of what He sends down – they say, 'You, [O Muhammad], are but an inventor [of lies].' But most of them do not know (Q 16:101 Sahih International).

This last verse acknowledges that Muhammad was accused of making up revelations and changing them to suit his purpose, and then claiming a doctrine of abrogation in his defence. Could not Allah have dictated a once and for all version of the Qur'an with no need for a law of abrogation, especially as traditionally, Muslims believe that the Qur'an 'came down' over a short period of time? Could this suggest that the Qur'an was written by authors who changed their minds?[147] According to Islamic tradition, it was Muhammad who received his revelations through a spirit being, which, after initial doubts, he decided was not Satan but an angel. This is not the only time that those around Muhammad wondered if there had been a demon or an angel around him.[148]

According to Islamic tradition, Muhammad did not write down the revelations. The Hadith tell us that multiple people wrote down the Qur'an – after some discussion as to whether it should be written down in the first place, and who should do this – partly because it was feared that parts of the Qur'an might otherwise be lost.[149]

Today there exists no complete Qur'an from the time it was supposed to have been compiled and written down.[150] And no versions of the Qur'ans today are exactly the same as the earliest versions of the Qur'an in existence.[151]

'Why does the Qur'an have abrogation if it was preserved by Allah in Heaven?'

It seems strange to the non-Muslim mind that Allah would include the law of abrogation in the Qur'an, given that the Qur'an is preserved with Allah. Presumably this means that Allah changed his mind before he even 'handed down'[152] 'the book' to Muhammad through the 'angel'.

If there had been no abrogation, then liberal Muslims could turn to the moderate verses, but must still contend with the many more that contradict those verses. It suggests that Allah had a change of opinion within his own revelation.

If verses were abrogated, then the 'peaceful' verses were abrogated by later verses which are seen as more authoritative,[153] coming from the last ten years of Muhammad's life, when his raids on non-Muslims gained prominence. The verses espousing violence are therefore authoritative today.

'What is your view of the 'Satanic Verses'?'

The 'Satanic verses' in the Qur'an were made famous by Salman Rushdie's book with this title.[154] According to Islamic tradition, some verses of the Qur'an (Q 53:19-20) were inspired by Satan.[155] This is clearly referred to in the Qur'an itself:

And We did not send before you any messenger or prophet except that when he spoke [or recited], Satan threw into it [some misunderstanding]. But Allah abolishes that which Satan throws in; then Allah makes precise His verses. And Allah is Knowing and Wise. [That is] so He may make what Satan throws in a trial for those within whose hearts is disease and those hard of heart. And indeed, the wrongdoers are in extreme dissension (Q 22:52-53 Sahih International).

The question arises as to whether any other verses were inspired by Satan, and why Allah allowed Muhammad to be inspired by Satan, given that he is the role model for all people, and to be obeyed (Q 33:45-46; 4:59). Why would Allah allow Satan to have inspired part of the preserved Qur'an, prior to it being given to Muhammad? If Allah permitted Satan to trick Muhammad, even though Q 15:9 tells us Allah protects his word, does it mean Allah is partnering with Satan, or that Satan was able to usurp Allah? If Satan has inspired some of it, then can any of it be trusted? Might this explain why the Qur'an opposes the life and work of the Saviour, Jesus?

These are very important questions that might be difficult for your Muslims friends to digest, but are invaluable to think through.

'The Qur'an commands obedience to Muhammad, (not just to Allah). Isn't this *shirk* (idolatry)?'

The Qur'an states implicitly that Muhammad should be cherished by Muslims as much as Allah.

Say, [O Muhammad], "If your fathers, your sons, your brothers, your wives, your relatives, wealth which you have obtained, commerce wherein you fear decline, and dwellings with which you are pleased are more beloved to you than Allah and His Messenger and jihad in His cause, then wait until Allah executes His command. And Allah does not guide the defiantly disobedient people" (Q 9:24 Sahih International).

Muslims are instructed to submit to Muhammad.

And whoever obeys Allah and the Messenger – those will be with the ones upon whom Allah has bestowed favor of the prophets, the steadfast affirmers of truth, the martyrs and the righteous. And excellent are those as companions (Q 4:69 Sahih International).

And obey Allah and obey the Messenger ...
(Q 5:92 Sahih International).

They are also told that their sins can be forgiven if they follow Muhammad and obey him alongside Allah.

Say [O Muhammad]: 'If ye do love Allah, Follow me: Allah will love you and forgive you your sins: For Allah is Oft-Forgiving, Most Merciful.' Say: 'Obey Allah and His Messenger': But if they turn back, Allah loveth not those who reject Faith (Q 3:31-32 Sahih International).

An objective reading of the Qur'an will lead you to conclude that Muhammad is so closely associated with Allah that he comes close to being divine. Islam strongly prohibits idolatry, which is called *shirk* in Islamic theology. Yet, might not venerating Muhammad (or the Qur'an) constitute a form of *shirk*?

If Allah is God, why would he allow a man to be obeyed alongside him, as if there were two deities? Is Muhammad trying to take the place of Christ? How could he?! Jesus is alive whereas Muhammad is in his grave; Muhammad cannot help us, whilst Jesus hears and helps us every day of our lives if we trust and call out to Him (Joel 2:32; Acts 2:21; Romans 10:6-13).

Christians don't obey or worship a mere man. We worship and obey God, which is why we love, obey, follow and worship Jesus. Jesus is fully divine and therefore worthy of worship and adoration.

This is an important point to make because Muslims believe that we commit *shirk* when we worship Jesus. Islamic theology misleads Muslims about who Jesus is, believing Christians to have taken a mere man and made him God. The Bible reveals Jesus as fully Man and fully God (see Genesis 3:8, 9; Genesis 17:1-4; Exodus 3; Numbers 12:8; 1 Samuel 3:10, 21; Matthew 1:23; Colossians 1:15).

9

Questions on Historical Inaccuracies in the Qur'an[156]

'Why does the Qur'an say that there were crucifixions in the time of the Pharaohs?'

The Qur'an relates the story of Moses asking permission for the people of Israel to go and worship. In the Qur'anic account, Pharaoh threatens to crucify them all:

> Said Pharaoh, 'You believed in him before I gave you permission. Indeed, this is a conspiracy which you conspired in the city to expel therefrom its people. But you are going to know. I will surely cut off your hands and your feet on opposite sides; then I will surely crucify you all' (Q 7:123-124 Sahih International). See also Q 20:71 and Q 26:49.

The Qur'an also relates something of the story of Joseph. In this passage Joseph is interpreting the dreams of his fellow prisoners and claims that one of them will be crucified.

> O two companions of prison, as for one of you, he will give drink to his master of wine; but as for the other, he will be crucified, and the birds will eat from his head. The matter has been decreed about which you both inquire (Q 12:41 Sahih International).

The Qur'an states in these verses that Pharaoh threatened punishment by crucifixion in the time of Joseph, circa 18th century BC - 17th century BC, and in the time of Moses, circa 16th century BC - 15th century BC.

There is no historical or archaeological evidence that the ancient Egyptians executed people by crucifixion in the 18th through to 15th centuries BC. The earliest recorded crucifixion was in 479 BC, by the Athenians, who crucified a Persian general named Artaÿctes. It was used by the Persians, also in the 5th century BC, and adopted by the Romans and others many hundreds of years after Joseph and Moses.[157] If the Qur'an is from God, why is it historically inaccurate?[158]

'Why does the Qur'an say that Joseph was sold for a few dirhams (coins)?'

Referring to the story in which Joseph is sold into slavery by his brothers, the Qur'an says:

> The (Brethren) sold him for a miserable price, for a few dirhams counted out: in such low estimation did they hold him! (Q 12:20 Yusuf Ali).

Dirhams did not exist in the time of Joseph. In fact, no coins existed then – and coins do not seem to appear in the archaeological record until around 700 BC.[159] If the Qur'an is from the 'all-knower', why did it get this so wrong? Does this suggest that the Qur'an is imperfect?

'Why does the Qur'an say that the golden calf was moulded by a Samaritan?'

In the story about the Israelites constructing a golden calf while Moses was receiving the Ten Commandments, the Qur'an claims that a Samaritan led the Israelites to manufacture the golden calf.

> (Allah) said: 'We have tested thy people in thy absence: the Samiri [Samaritan] has led them astray' (Q 20:85 Yusuf Ali).

> They said: 'We broke not the promise to thee, as far as lay in our power: but we were made to carry the weight of the ornaments of the (whole) people, and we threw them (into the fire), and that was what the Samiri [Samaritan] suggested' (Q 20:87 Yusuf Ali; see also Q 20:95).

The city of Samaria was not founded until the 9th century BC, when King Omri built it (1 Kings 16:24). The Samaritan people emerged after the importation of conquered people into the districts of Samaria (2 Kings 17:24-41). Modern English translations try to avoid translating the Arabic word 'Samaritan' and use 'Samiri' instead, without any basis in the Arabic.[160] Why does the Qur'an get this point of history so wrong?

'Why are there so many errors of historicity in the Qur'an?'
We have shown, through a number of examples, that the Qur'an lacks historical authenticity. Why is this, if the Qur'an is supposed to be an eternal or preserved document dictated by the angel Gabriel? If Allah is god, why is he unaware of the facts of history?

'Why does the Qur'an say that Jews believe Ezra is the son of God?'

> The Jews say, 'Ezra is the son of Allah'; and the Christians say, 'The Messiah is the son of Allah.' That is their statement from their mouths; they imitate the saying of those who disbelieved [before them]. May Allah destroy them; how are they deluded? (Q 9:30 Sahih International).

Some translations say 'Uzair', or an alternative spelling that is identified with Ezra. In fact, Jews have never believed that Ezra is the son of God.[161]

'Why is Mary, the mother of Isa, the only woman mentioned in the Qur'an by name?'
Mary [or Maryam in Arabic], the mother of Isa in the Qur'an, is the only named woman in the Qur'an. Her name appears thirty-four times.[162] Why is this honour given to Mary, and not to the mother of Muhammad? This is probably not a life-changing conversation. However, it might force your Muslim friend to consider the importance of Isa, whom they believe to be Jesus.

The concept of Isa in the Qur'an has kept many Muslims from believing in Jesus. That said, you may hear testimonies from Muslims who have left Islam to follow Jesus as God, after seeing Him in a vision. In some of these visions He will introduce Himself by the name 'Isa'. This is not to say that He is identifying with the

Qur'anic Isa on any level. He is introducing Himself to Muslims who genuinely think that Isa is Jesus. He then shows them who He really is. After such visions, most Muslims will need to meet a Christian or read the Bible before leaving Islam to follow Jesus – a different person and One far greater than the Isa of the Qur'an.

According to the Qur'an, the father of Mary, Isa's mother, was called Imran (Sura 3:33). According to the Bible, Imran, or Amram, was the father of Miriam, the sister of Moses. They lived hundreds of years before Isa.

Let's now ask some questions about the formation of the Qur'an and what the earliest extant copies of the Qur'an tell us.

'Why are there differences between the earliest Qur'ans?'
This question will require further study, and you will need to be able to provide evidence to support what you say. However, Muslims are beginning to doubt, and leave Islam due to this fast-emerging area of study.[163]

This is an important question because Muslims believe that the Qur'an is preserved unchanged (Q 85:22), and was complete by the time of the third ruler (Caliph) after Muhammad, during mid-7th century – in 652 AD. This is within twenty years of Muhammad's death.

According to Islamic tradition, five Qur'ans were sent by Uthman as models, to five cities in 652 AD. Yet, not one exists today – anywhere – and it takes another century before we find manuscripts which are the closest to those attributed to Uthman (see Bukhari V6, bk61, h509-510).

There are a handful of early Qur'ans, that are not in agreement with each other. Here are six of them (note their dates):

1. Topkapi (Istanbul, early to mid-8th century)[164]
2. Sammarqand (Tashkent, early to mid-8th century)[165]
3. Al Husseini (Cairo, early to mid-8th century)[166]
4. Paris Petropolitanus (Paris, early 8th century)[167]
5. Ma'il (London, late 8th century)[168]
6. Sana'a (early 8th century)[169]

If the Islamic claim that the Qur'an originated in mid-7th century is to be believed, then we should expect to see Qur'ans from that period onwards, which are uniform and unchanged. Yet not even one exists from that time, and none of the earliest existing Qur'ans agree with one other.

'Are you aware that there are multiple versions of *Arabic* Qur'ans in existence today?'

Most Muslims are not aware that the modern Qur'an was only finalised in 1924, in Cairo. And even then, over thirty-one different versions of Arabic Qur'ans exist today. They are not uniform and have upwards of ninety-three thousand differences between them.[170]

Even more disturbing is the fact that the official 1924 'Hafs' text, which is considered to be the standard text for the majority of Muslims today, is attributed to a student named 'Hafs', who lived in Kufa (d. 796 AD). He could not, therefore, have had contact with Muhammad since he was born 74 years after Muhammad died, and hundreds of miles away at that. Surprisingly, one can buy as many as seven different 'Hafs' versions of the Qur'an in the Arabic-speaking world today.

'Why does the Qur'an misrepresent Christian theology?'

The Qur'an depicts Mary, the mother of Jesus, as a member of the Trinity.

> And behold! Allah will say: 'O Jesus the son of Mary! Didst thou say unto men, worship me and my mother as gods in derogation of Allah?' (Q 5:116 Yusuf Ali).

> O People of the Book! Commit no excesses in your religion: Nor say of Allah aught but the truth. Christ Jesus the son of Mary was (no more than) a messenger of Allah, and His Word, which He bestowed on Mary, and a spirit proceeding from Him: so believe in Allah and His messengers. Say not 'Trinity': desist: it will be better for you: for Allah is one Allah: Glory be to Him: (far exalted is He) above having a son. To Him belong all things in the heavens and

on earth. And enough is Allah as a Disposer of affairs"
(Q 4:171 Yusuf Ali).

The Qur'an also depicts the Trinity as three separate gods rather
than one united God who is three persons.

> Surely, disbelievers are those who said: 'Allah is the third
> of the three (in a Trinity).' But there is no ilah (god) but One
> Ilah (God-Allah). And if they cease not from what they say,
> verily, a painful torment will befall the disbelievers among
> them (Q 5:73 Muhsin Khan).

(See also Q 5:116, which conveys the erroneous idea that the
'Christian' God is made up of three gods, including Mary.)

Christians do not believe that Mary is a member of the
Trinity. Nor do they believe that the Trinity is comprised of three
gods.[171] The authors of the Qur'an were clearly mistaken in their
understanding of Christianity. We know this simply by comparing
it to Biblical truth. Nowhere in the Bible is it suggested that Mary
is divine, which means that Q 4:171 is incorrect. Similarly, Q 5:73
shows no understanding of the Trinity.

'How do you prove that the Qur'an came from God?'

We have shown earlier that the Qur'an lacks historical authenticity.
Furthermore, it includes no examples of fulfilled prophecies.[172]
The Qur'an claims to authenticate itself by being incomparable:

> And if you are in doubt about what We have sent down [i.e.,
> the Qur'an] upon Our Servant [Muhammad], then produce a
> surah the like thereof and call upon your witnesses other than
> Allah, if you should be truthful (Q 2:23 Sahih International).

> Say, "If mankind and the jinn gathered in order to produce
> the like of this Qur'an, they could not produce the like of
> it, even if they were to each other assistants" (Q 17:88; See
> also Q 10:37-38 Sahih International).

Because of this verse, your Muslim friends will often challenge
you to present 'a sura like it'. Some have taken up this challenge

and compared the Qur'an with other genres of literature.[173] If you are asked to produce a passage that is comparable with the Qur'an,[174] we suggest that you read your favourite passage from the Bible, or, for example, Exodus 3, Psalm 8, Psalm 23, the Beatitudes, 1 Corinthians 13 or Revelation 5. You could also ask them to find a sura like those verses in the Bible. We are confident that the Bible points us to the Eternal Word of God, who transforms lives (Hebrews 4:12-15).

If we truly believe that the Gospel has the power to change lives and society, then we have a confidence and boldness that our Muslim friends need to see. They may be confident, yet their foundation is weak, while we can be confident because our foundation is strong. The historical accuracy and many remarkable fulfilled prophecies of the Bible validate its reliability. The Bible is an accurate portrayal of the events of history, including 'embarrassing' stories, true to normal human experience. It has withstood extensive historical criticism and challenges from sceptics.[175] Its historical accuracy points to its reliability, indicating that its message should be taken seriously.

So, what reasons can be provided for believing the Qur'an? Does the Qur'an stand up to historical critique? What does the archaeological record tell us about the claims of Islam?[176]

10

Questions Muslims Ask

Throughout this book so far, you will have read different responses you might receive from those who disagree with you. However, there are specific questions that arise repeatedly in conversation with Muslims that are worthy of attention. They are pertinent questions, designed to generate meaningful conversations. You too may have asked some of them as you journeyed towards accepting Jesus as your Lord and Saviour. God loves us to 'seek Him' – something which is not encouraged in other religions. He calls people to Himself: 'And you will seek Me and find Me, when you search for me with all your heart. I will be found by you, says the Lord ...' (Jeremiah 29:13-14). This invitation is reiterated in Jesus' renowned Sermon on the Mount: 'For everyone who asks receives, and he who seeks finds, and to him who knocks it will be opened' (Matthew 7:8).

In the next section, we introduce the most common questions that Muslims ask Christians.

'How can God have a Son?'

For Christians, the title 'Son of God' is primarily a relational divine title.[177] From all eternity He has always been the divine Son of the Father, and He always will be. Through Jesus, the divine and human Son, God is revealed to human beings. He is the seen face of God (Exodus 33:11; Numbers 12:8). If you know Jesus, you know the Father (John 7:28, 14:7). The Son is the image of the invisible God, the Firstborn over all creation ... All things were created through Him and for Him (see Colossians 1:15; Philippians 2:5-11; Hebrews 1:1-3).

One of the most astounding revelations from God the Father is this: when Jesus was baptised, the heavens were opened and the Spirit of God descended on Jesus like a dove. Then the Father spoke from heaven, saying: "This is My beloved Son, in whom I am well pleased" (Matthew 3:16-17).

The Bible tells us that the Son reveals the Father.

"All things have been delivered to Me by My Father, and no one knows the Son except the Father. Nor does anyone know the Father except the Son, and the one to whom the Son wills to reveal Him" (Matthew 11:27).

For a Muslim this is difficult to grasp. In part, this is because Allah is a singular entity – a higher power that is not given such personal familial names. Allah is not 'Abba Father' to Muslims. Allah is not a Trinity, and more problematic for Muslims is the Qur'anic insistence that Allah does not have a son (Q 6:101; 39:4 – although the latter verse does acknowledge the possibility of it). To the Muslim way of thinking, Sonship refers to a biological son, a created being, with no consideration to the fact that that Sonship means so much more in Biblical thinking.

The Qur'an takes great pains to make clear that Allah has no sons or daughters:

But they have attributed to Allah partners – the jinn, while He has created them – and have fabricated for Him sons and daughters without knowledge. Exalted is He and high above what they describe (Q 6:100 Sahih International).

This verse may be challenging local pagan thought, or Greek mythology, rather than the Bible, since the Bible never presents a daughter as part of the Godhead. Q 39:4 implies that Allah could take a son from his creation. The Qur'an doesn't allow for the possibility of an *eternal* Son, uncreated, who, alongside the Father and Holy Spirit, created us and the world (Genesis 1:1-3; 1:26-27; Proverbs 8:26-30; Colossians 1:16; Hebrews 1:2).

If someone objects to the Father, Son and Holy Spirit – the eternal God – just take them back to Scripture. All through the Bible we see the Father, Son and the Holy Spirit moving and working in creation and redemption.

A good place to start is the Epistle to the Hebrews. Become familiar with it, work through the book, heading back into all the

Old Testament passages it quotes, and read them through with your Muslim friends. It will be balm for your soul, as it presents the Lord Jesus for who He is, leading you through to the amazing verses of Hebrews 11:1-12:3, which tell us about the Old and New Testament believers who trusted in the Lord who died for us.

'Did God have sex with Mary?'

This is a very odd question for the Christian, as our Scriptures are clear on the miraculous conception of Jesus in the womb of Mary. Remember also that Jesus existed before He was born. His conception was supernatural. A bigger and more profound question would be 'How and why would a pre-existent God choose to become a baby in a womb?' Muslims do ask this question and it is a great question! They may point to the word 'beget/begotten' in the Bible:

> *For God so loved the world that He gave His only begotten Son, that whoever believes in Him should not perish but have everlasting life'* (John 3 :16).

Muslims may try to impose a narrow definition of the word 'begotten' to try to prove that Jesus was only a human being. But 'begotten' also means 'given' or 'caused', and this word cannot be used to limit Jesus' identity to 'just a human being'. Jesus' Sonship was and is unique *because* he was begotten, whilst Christians are not conceived miraculously but are adopted by God as sons and daughters. The angel said to Mary:

> *"...you will conceive in your womb and bring forth a Son, and shall call His name Jesus. He will be great, and will be called the Son of the highest; and the Lord God will give Him the throne of His father David. And He will reign over the House of Jacob forever, and of His kingdom there will be no end"* (Luke 1:31-33).

Jesus is the given Son, who pre-existed, and who is the Creator of us all (Genesis 1:26-27; John 1:1-14; Colossians 1:15-16; Hebrews 1:1-3).

111

This question is a problem for Islam rather than Christianity. The Qur'an provides a story of how Allah made a chaste girl called Maryam pregnant. A spirit appeared in the form of a man (Q 19:17) and breathed into her to make her pregnant (Q 19:17-21; Q 21:91; Q 66:12). It is a strange anomaly in the Qur'an, and makes the figure of 'Isa' miraculous.

The Bible tells us that the Holy Spirit caused Mary to conceive. Many ask 'how' this is. No one can answer 'how' God does something unless He reveals it to us, and the Bible always provides us with insight:

> *The angel answered and said to her, "The Holy Spirit will come upon you, and the power of the Highest will overshadow you; therefore, also, that Holy One who is to be born will be called the Son of God"* (Luke 1:35).

'How can human beings be made in God's Image?'

Consider this: you are made in the image of God! This means you have intrinsic value and purpose and the potential for an eternal life, lived free from pain, confusion and struggle. It also means that we have a God who understands us and who can relate to us directly.

Islam distances Allah from creation. It places a veil between him and humankind. Anyone accepting this view would find it difficult to believe that we were made in God's image since Allah is fundamentally unknowable. A human being in the image of God makes little sense to Muslims. If you are asked this question, it is a great opportunity to tease out these differences between Allah and the Lord God of the Bible.

'How can God become a man?'

A witty person might quickly respond, "You mean Allah can't?!", because the question highlights an issue with the Islamic view of god rather than the Biblical. The great divide in the theology of god between Christians and Muslims is highlighted here. Allah never has, nor can, become a man. This is the polar opposite of the Lord of the Bible, in whose image all human beings are made.

Let's unpack this question further. The very need to ask 'how' shows us that we are merely human. If we knew all the 'hows' then we would be God. What we do know is that God has often appeared to people in history, and will continue to do so (Genesis 3:8-9,18; Exodus 3:14-16; Numbers 12:8; Revelation 1:12-18; Revelation 19; Revelation 21:1-4). God walking and talking with human beings is what He has done throughout history.

The Bible is clear about who this person is – He is Jesus.

He is the image of the invisible God, the firstborn over all creation. For by Him all things were created that are in heaven and that are on earth, visible and invisible, whether thrones or dominions or principalities or powers. All things were created through Him and for Him. And He is before all things, and in Him all things consist (Colossians 1:15-17).

To understand this further, why not ponder and share the following list of verses:

- Genesis 3:8-9 shows God walking with Adam and Eve in the garden of Eden. We read that they 'heard' the LORD walking through the garden. Genesis 16 tells us the story of Hagar who, after she met 'The Angel of the LORD', declared: "You are the God who sees ...."

- Genesis 18 tells us of the LORD speaking with Abraham in person – He sat down to eat a meal with Abraham.

- Exodus 3:1-15 gives the account of God speaking directly with Moses, introducing Himself by His personal names, "I AM WHO I AM", "Thus you shall say to the children of Israel, 'The LORD God [Yahweh] of your fathers, the God of Abraham, the God of Isaac and the God of Jacob, has sent me to you. This is My name forever and this is My memorial to all generations.'"

- See also Exodus 33:11: *'So the LORD spoke to Moses face to face, as a man speaks to his friend.'*

- Numbers 12:8 has God telling us that Moses sees His form: *"I speak with him face to face, even plainly, and not in dark sayings; and he sees the form of the LORD..."*

- 1 Samuel 3:10, 21 tells us: *'Now the LORD came and stood and called as at other times, "Samuel! Samuel!" And Samuel answered, "Speak, for Your servant hears." Then the LORD appeared again in Shiloh. For the LORD revealed Himself to Samuel in Shiloh by the Word of the LORD.'*

- John 1:18 informs us: *'No one has seen God at any time. The only begotten Son, who is in the bosom of the Father, He has declared Him'.*

- Daniel 7:13-14 tells us about the *'Son of Man'*, the man of heaven approaching *'the Ancient of Days'*. Here we catch a glimpse of the throne room of heaven, with the Father and the Son.[178]

- Matthew 1:21-23 clearly communicates who Jesus is: *"And she will bring forth a Son, and you shall call His name Jesus, for He will save His people from their sins." So all this was done that it might be fulfilled which was spoken by the Lord through the prophet, saying: "Behold, the virgin shall be with child, and bear a Son, and they shall call His name Immanuel," which is translated, 'God with us'.*

- Hebrews 1:1-4 points to the Son being *'the express image'* of God – the One through whom God speaks.

Revelation 5:6-14 reveals the slain Lamb, worshipped by every tribe and tongue. This is important, as Islamic texts deny that Jesus died on a cross. This verse is also helpful to show other divine titles of Jesus and His sacrifice for humanity.

When we let the Scriptures speak for themselves about who the Lord Jesus is, many of our doubts are dispelled. For example, Revelation 19 shows us the leader of God's armies – the Host of Heaven – standing as a heavenly man ready for battle, and dealing with evil once and for all. We are given a clear description of who Jesus is, what He does and how we should refer to Him:

He was clothed with a robe dipped in blood, and His name is called The Word of God. And the armies in heaven, clothed in fine linen, white and clean, followed Him on white horses. Now out of His mouth goes a sharp sword, that with it He should strike the nations. And He Himself will rule them with a rod of iron. He Himself treads the winepress of the fierceness and wrath of Almighty God. And He has on His robe and on His thigh a name written: 'KING OF KINGS AND LORD OF LORDS' (Revelation 19:13-16).

And of course never forget the wonderful promises of Revelation 21:3-6, which tells us of God living with us and personally removing pain and death from us.

It is a delight to walk our Muslim friends through the Bible, revealing the Living God throughout.[179]

'Why do you believe in three gods?'

Christians do not believe in three gods. We believe in one God: Father, Son and Holy Spirit. God is a relational being. By contrast, Allah is described as *Tawhid* in Islamic theology. *Tawhid* contains the concept of 'singularity' – a simple one (Q 4:171). Allah is therefore seen as a singular entity that is indivisible, one unit that is untouchable, and an entity that does not enter our realm in any physical manifestation. Allah is a monad with no relatability. Creation has no connection with Allah in the thinking of most Muslims. The Trinity, by contrast, shows that the Living God is fundamentally relational.

The account of the baptism of Jesus, including the Holy Spirit descending and alighting on Him, and the voice of the Father from Heaven expressing pleasure with His beloved Son (Matthew 3:13-17), is a helpful study to share with Muslims, as are Genesis 1, John 1, Colossians 1 and Hebrews 1. In these verses the Father, Son, and Holy Spirit, their eternal life and their work in history is shown.

'Has the Bible been corrupted?'

Muslims are taught that the Bible has been corrupted. In fact, there are manuscripts of the Bible that pre-date the Qur'an by hundreds of years. What evidence is there for the alleged corruption of the Bible? At what time in history was the Bible changed? You could ask if your friend could show you which parts have been changed. Was it before or after the Qur'an? The historical evidence clearly supports a reliable text of the Bible.[180] Even the Qur'an testifies to the inspiration of the Bible at the time of Muhammad.[181] The Qur'an does not say that the Bible has been corrupted, so when did this idea enter Islamic thinking? Was it from the time of Muhammad or much later? It is very likely to have been a challenge posed to Christians when Muslims conquered Christian lands. When we consider history, we see an increase in challenges against Christianity after Islam's invasion of Christian Spain. A Muslim historian called Ibn Hazm introduced the challenge in the 11th century; it is not seen in Islamic literature before then.[182]

When a Muslim claims that the Bible has been corrupted, ask these three questions: When? Where? By whom? Some Muslims will point to the Council of Nicaea. Misinformed on this, some believe that this is when the Trinity, and the divinity of Jesus, were 'invented', and the Bible completed. This challenge has been thoroughly discredited by the writings of the Church Fathers who delved deeply into the theology of the Bible, as well as by thousands of Biblical manuscripts and fragments. No text accepted by the early Church denies Jesus as God, and none deny the Trinity. The Bible existed before the Council of Nicaea in 325 AD. It may not have been in the form of a single book, but the various books and letters were first circulated amongst the churches, affirmed in their teaching, and then directly quoted by the Church Fathers and Saints throughout history.

'Why are Christian countries so corrupt?'

Sadly, 'Christian' countries are not inhabited by sinless people, nor are past Christian values always evident. Humanity is deeply flawed, meaning we will not be able to set up a perfect community this side of eternity. We should nevertheless continually strive for peace and justice here on earth. History confirms that societies founded on Biblical laws and morals have been more successful in achieving this compared with societies founded on alternative belief systems.

The fact that some Western countries influenced by Christianity in the past generally expose corruption and can question it publicly, speaks to the accountability which Christianity demands of human rulers.[183] Perhaps it is one reason why many people still strive to come to the West rather than flee to Muslim nations, some of which are far more wealthy than many Western nations. That said, we see in the 21st century, profound intolerance, coupled with the rejection of Christian values in much of Western society. If left to continue unbridled without a sudden wake up call, society will continue its march towards corruption and depravity, which ultimately destroys life. Many Muslims understand this, and believe that Islamic law (the Shariah) is the answer; yet this is just as oppressive as extreme secular regimes, and does not bring true freedom. Some Muslims do not agree with Islamic law, and instead have adopted secular pluralism, which also ultimately leads to oppressive regimes, as we have begun to see in some sectors of modern society, where conservative family values are reviled.[184]

What is the antidote to oppressive regimes? Where do we find true freedom?[185]

God's freedom is not a law, it is not a concept, nor is it an ideology. True freedom is found in the person who paved the way to enable us to live with God: the risen, Living Lord Jesus – the Son of God. Citizens are most likely to flourish in societies built on Christian values.

'What about the Crusades?'

Why do you think the Crusades happened? Was it a conquest? Was it revenge? Was it for justice? Was it to protect the vulnerable? Were they just? Is it ever right for leaders of countries to wage war in response to unjust atrocities or tyrannical invasions? What if this was the main reason for the Crusades?

Until recent times, it was well-recognised that the Crusades arose after four hundred years of Islamic aggression and the persecution of Christians and other groups. The Islamic conquests swept through Africa to Europe, the Middle East, and through Asia. Great Christian cities had been destroyed and Christians were massacred or brought into submission as the Islamic armies invaded. Christians in the conquered lands pleaded for help from other nations.

Take, for example, the cruelty of Abd Al-Rahman III (also called al-Nasir), an Islamic leader in Spain. He reigned from 912 AD to 929 AD. One particular report of barbarity informs us that one hundred Christians were executed in front of him while he was on holiday, and their execution celebrated in a poem:

> ... defeated, the prisoners arrived, carried and shackled by Allah ... in plain sight of everyone your sword annihilated them, among blessing and praises to Allah ...[186]

Islamic leaders like Abd Al-Rahman III were not an exception – many Caliphs were like him. They were encouraged by laws which supported barbaric abuses of citizens in the nations dominated by the Islamic conquests. We know that Islam spread through conquest from Islamic sources such as the biographies[187] and the histories of Islam.[188] We also know what happened from eyewitness accounts, including those from the Crusaders, recorded in medieval writings.[189]

Individual Christians and churches have carried out acts which God would not endorse. This does not mean that Christianity condones murder. It is difficult, however, for a Muslim to say that Islam does not call for the murder, terrorisation and suppression of non-Muslims, when Qur'anic verses such as Q 5:33, 8:12 and 47:4 provide clear evidence for these. These are verses that do not relate to a particular time period or event but rather, have a timeless feature to them.

> Remember thy Lord inspired the angels (with the message): 'I am with you: give firmness to the Believers: I will instil terror into the hearts of the Unbelievers: smite ye above their necks and smite all their finger-tips off them (Q 8:12 Yusuf Ali).

Many of our Muslim friends would not support murder or terror, yet they do not know what their texts say. Knowing what our respective texts teach is important for knowing the truth so that we may choose wisely for the betterment of our families and society.

'Who is Jesus?'

The wonderful descriptions of the Lord Jesus in Revelation 19 should cause us to pause in awe as we consider Him to be 'the Word of God', the 'King of kings and Lord of lords' who will conquer all evil. King Jesus is the Heavenly Warrior who rules over the armies of Heaven and will live with those who love and trust Him as their Lord and Saviour.

> '... the tabernacle of God is with men, and He will dwell with them, and they shall be His people. God Himself will be with them and be their God. And God will wipe away every tear from their eyes; there shall be no more death, nor sorrow, nor crying. There shall be no more pain, for the former things have passed away.' Then He who sat on the throne said, 'Behold, I make all things new' (Revelation 21:3-5).

Jesus is not only a prophet, or someone to admire. He is also God, as is so clearly presented in the Bible. His death achieved salvation for everyone who places their trust in Him. His resurrection demonstrates His power. He should be worshipped and adored.

'Did Jesus say the Old Testament speaks of Him?'

Ponder these verses in Luke 24:44. Jesus tells His disciples that Moses, the Prophets and the Psalms speak of Him:

> "These are the words which I spoke to you while I was still with you, that all things must be fulfilled which were written in the Law of Moses and the Prophets and the Psalms concerning Me."

That means our Creator, the Lord Jesus, is written about throughout the laws of Moses, the Prophets and the Psalms.

> "For if you believed Moses, you would believe Me; for he wrote about me. But if you do not believe his writings, how will you believe My words?" (John 5:46-47).

This becomes particularly important when discussing our faith with Muslims because the Qur'an omits this foundational teaching from its version of the history of Moses.

When we share about the Lord's work in history it can be helpful to point to His creative, protecting, leading and guiding work. God is present, is working and is active (Colossians 1:15; Hebrews 1:1-3). As you read the following verses ask yourself who, specifically, these verses are about:

"I am the LORD [Yahweh] *your God, Who brought you out of the land of Egypt"* (Psalm 81:10).

God protects His people:

To Him who led His people through the wilderness, For His mercy endures forever; To Him who struck down great kings, For His mercy endures forever (Psalm 136:16-17).[190]

King David testified of Jesus:

For David says concerning Him [Jesus] *"I foresaw the Lord always before my face. For He is at my right hand, that I may not be shaken; therefore my heart rejoiced, and my tongue was glad..."* (Acts 2:25-26).

David did not see Jesus as a distant, unknowable being. Rather, he praises Him for being next to him and before him. King David spoke of Jesus' death and resurrection a thousand years beforehand:

"... of the patriarch David, he... foreseeing this, spoke concerning the resurrection of the Christ, that His soul was not left in Hades, nor did His flesh see corruption. This Jesus God has raised up, of which we are all witnesses" (Acts 2:29, 31-32).

This passage is quoting from Psalm 16:10: *"For You will not leave my soul in Sheol, Nor will You allow Your Holy One to see corruption."*

Consider also, the words of Jesus as he was dying on the cross – words written one thousand years earlier in Psalm 22:1:

"My God, My God, why have You forsaken Me? Why are You so far from helping Me, And from the words of My groaning?"

Jesus knows He is divine, and knows the Father:

"It is My Father who honours Me, of whom you say that He is your God. Yet you have not known Him, but I know Him. And if I say, 'I do not know Him,' I shall be a liar like you; but I do know Him and keep His word. Your father Abraham rejoiced to see My day, and he saw it and was glad… most assuredly, I say to you, before Abraham was, I AM" (John 8:54-58).

Jesus existed before the creation of the world. As Jesus prayed[191] to His Father [192] he mentions the glory He had with the Him before the world began:

"O Father, glorify Me together with Yourself, with the glory which I had with You before the world was" (John 17:5).

We are given many glimpses into the magnificence of the glory of the seen Yahweh throughout the Scriptures. Marvel at the depth of theology, and the beauty of the seen face of God – reported by Moses in Exodus 24:9-18. Who, specifically, did Moses and the leaders see?

Then Moses went up, also Aaron, Nadab, and Abihu, and seventy of the elders of Israel, and they saw the God of Israel. And there was under His feet as it were a paved work of sapphire stone and it was like the very heavens in its clarity. But on the nobles of the children of Israel He did not lay His hand. So they saw God, and they ate and drank. Then the LORD said to Moses, 'Come up to me on the mountain and be there; and I will give you tablets of stone, and the law and commandments which I have written, that you may teach them'… Now the glory of the LORD rested on Mount Sinai… The sight of the glory of the LORD was like a consuming fire on the top of the mountain in the eyes of the children of Israel. So Moses went into the midst of the cloud and went up into the mountain.

Many people ask how we speak of the Lord Jesus with those who believe God is an elusive and unknown being? Your first step is simply to let His written word speak for itself. Exodus 24 not only gives us a view of Heaven, but it also shows God communing with the elders of His people, enjoying a banquet with them. We read of God giving His laws to Moses in person. The Lord's glory is then seen by all the people.

Let Scripture speak for itself. Nothing in these passages describes the god of Islam or any other religious view of god, and they present a challenging perspective for those who do not believe.[193]

'Do the Old and New Testaments teach the same about Jesus?'
There was no New Testament at the time of Pentecost – the day when the Holy Spirit filled the Apostles and followers of Jesus, just as Jesus had promised (John 14:15-17; John 16:13-16). Peter, filled with the Holy Spirit, taught the crowds at the temple about Jesus from the Old Testament, referencing the writings of prophets including Joel and King David.

The Epistle to the Hebrews in particular, makes extensive use of the Old Testament, illuminating many Old Testament passages. Hebrews chapters 11 through to 12 show the clear and continuous experience of the faith of Old Testament believers, given to us as examples to follow. Those Old Testament saints were waiting for the same city built by the same God, as Christians today (Hebrews 11:10), but, more importantly, are commended for having the same trust in the same God.

By faith Moses rejected the wealth and luxury of Egypt *'for he endured as seeing Him who is invisible'*[194] (Hebrews 11:27). Rahab did not die with those who disbelieved, but was rescued because she believed (Hebrews 11:31). Many were miraculously preserved in life, others tortured to death, but they all waited for the same promise as us *'that they should not be made perfect apart from us'* (Hebrews 11:40). It is their witness that we are to look to when we consider Jesus, and like them, persevere, because Jesus is the author of their faith and ours. He is the example for all of us to follow because only He has endured the cross, its shame, and is now seated at the right hand of the Father (Hebrews 12:1-3). Believers before and after the cross worship the same God:

> *Therefore since we are surrounded by so great a cloud of witnesses, let us lay aside every weight, and the sin which so easily ensnares us, and let us run with endurance the race that is set before us, looking unto Jesus, the author and finisher of our faith, who for the joy that was set before Him endured the cross, despising the shame, and has sat down at the right hand of the throne of God...* (Hebrews 12:1-2).

Hebrews 4:2 elaborates on the same theme: '*For indeed the gospel was preached to us as well as to them.*' Who is '*them*' in this verse? '*Them*' refers to the people living with Moses in the desert (Hebrews 3:16-19 and the book of Exodus). Consider what other New Testament writers say of Jesus:

> *He* [Jesus] *was in the beginning... all things were made through Him...* (John 1:2-3).

> *...by Him* [Jesus] *all things were created...* (Colossians 1:16).

> *God* [the Father] *through Him* [Jesus] *made the worlds* (Hebrews 1:2)

> *...I* [Jesus] *make all things new, I am the ...beginning and the end* (Revelation 21:5).

It all starts and ends with Jesus! Most Christians know that the world was made through God's Word, but be clear on what that Word is – it is not just a voice, it is a Person! The Living Lord Jesus (John 1:1-3, 14-18).

'Is the Gospel in the Old Testament?'
Absolutely. The New Testament makes clear that the Old Testament teaches salvation through the Lord Jesus Christ. A charge is given to a young man called Timothy to hold fast to the Scriptures he was raised with, which made him '*wise for salvation through faith which is in Christ Jesus*' (2 Timothy 3:15). Which Scriptures is it referring to? The New Testament had not yet been written. It is the

Old Testament which gives Timothy wisdom for salvation in the Lord Jesus Christ.

> *But you must continue in the things which you have learned and been assured of, knowing from whom you have learned them, and that from childhood you have known the Holy Scriptures, which are able to make you wise for salvation through faith which is in Christ Jesus. All Scripture is given by inspiration of God, and is profitable for doctrine, for reproof, for correction, for instruction in righteousness, that the man of God may be complete, thoroughly equipped for every good work* (2 Timothy 3:14-17).

The entire Old Testament testifies to the salvation and rescue mission of God. The prophets speak of God's love and mercy and forgiveness, but also his judgment. They foretell the coming Messiah and a new covenant.

> *"Behold, the days are coming," says the Lord, "when I will make a new covenant with the house of Israel and with the house of Judah— not according to the covenant that I made with their fathers in the day that I took them by the hand to lead them out of the land of Egypt, My covenant which they broke, though I was a husband to them, says the Lord...for they all shall know Me, from the least of them to the greatest of them," says the Lord ... "For I will forgive their iniquity, and their sin I will remember no more"* (Jeremiah 31:31-34).

God calls His people to remember how He rescued them throughout history. He reminds His people of His miraculous rescue out of slavery and bondage (Deuteronomy 5:6; Joshua 24:17; Psalm 136:10-11; Daniel 9:15; Amos 3:1; Micah 6:4). Out of slavery He leads the church to the city He has prepared for them (Hebrews 11:16). During this time the sacrificial system points to the cross. From both we learn that it is impossible to approach a holy God unless our sins are dealt with. It will take Jesus' death to provide the solution. God's sacrifice is seen through the animal skin coverings given to Adam and Eve (Genesis 3:21), The Lord's covenant with Abram – which the Lord alone could establish (Genesis 15), Abraham's willingness to sacrifice his son Isaac, and God's provision of a ram to die in his place (Genesis 22:10-14). All these point to the cross on which Jesus would die as the ultimate sacrifice (Matthew 27:32-56; Acts 2:22-33; Hebrews 1:3, 2:17-18).

'If Jesus is a warrior who will lead his people into battle, doesn't that make him violent?'

Reflect on Jesus' ministry when he lived on earth. During this time, Jesus never led His followers into battle. In fact, He criticised Peter when he used a sword to defend Him, and healed the high priest's servant, whose ear Peter had cut off (John 18:10-11). This is in sharp contrast to the life of Muhammad. Jesus went on to feel and experience the raw, corrupt violence of humanity against Him. He chose to endure the cross because He knew His sacrifice was needed to rescue humanity (John 15:13; Romans 5:8-10; 1 Peter 2:22-24).

The word 'violence' is used only with negative connotations today. Yet the Bible makes clear that kings are in place to police and keep the peace of nations. Security forces need to use force in times of war and danger. *'For rulers are not a terror to good works, but to evil'* (Romans 13:3). Rulers should strike fear into those who do evil. This should be the case with the law courts of the land, judges and prisons. A ruler is to be *'God's minister to you for good'*. Rulers are *'avengers to execute wrath on him who practices evil'* (Romans 13:4).

Deep down, most people recognise that there is a need for justice. When people experience a flagrant injustice, they naturally protest that it is unfair. In doing so they are appealing to a natural sense of justice. Our concepts of justice can be flawed because of our sinful nature and our lack of complete knowledge. But God has a perfectly just nature and has perfect knowledge of all circumstances. Only He, therefore, is able to administer perfect justice. In the light of eternity, all His judgments will be seen to have been perfectly fair and righteous. He will not allow sin to go unpunished, or evil to be left undefeated. This means that when He leads into battle, his character of goodness, love and righteousness is fully informed to make correct judgements.

What is more, Jesus is also the Alpha and the Omega (Revelation 1:8). Everything, including life, starts and ends with Him (Genesis 1; John 1; Revelation 19:21). He is the Head of the armies of Heaven – this is the meaning of 'LORD of Hosts' (Joshua 5:13-15; Revelation 19:11-16). He is the One who sits on the throne, the One whose dominion will never end (Daniel 7:9-14), and the One whose Judgment Seat we will stand before one day (Romans 14:10; Revelation 22:12). He has rescued us, and He removes our sins from us (Psalm 103:12).

To sum up, this is how Jesus described Himself and His ministry:

"The Spirit of the Lord God is upon Me,
Because the Lord has anointed Me
To preach good tidings to the poor;
He has sent Me to heal the brokenhearted,
To proclaim liberty to the captives,
And the opening of the prison to those who are bound;
To proclaim the acceptable year of the Lord,
And the day of vengeance of our God;
To comfort all who mourn,
To console those who mourn in Zion,
To give them beauty for ashes,
The oil of joy for mourning,
The garment of praise for the spirit of heaviness;
That they may be called trees of righteousness,
The planting of the Lord, that He may be glorified."

(Isaiah 61:1-3; Luke 4:18-21)

Notes

[1] There is a full list in Zuck, Roy B. 1995. *Teaching as Jesus Taught* (Baker Books: Grand Rapids, Michigan) (pp. 258-276).

[2] Qur'anic references can be found online at quran.com or corpus.quran.com. Quotations in this book are from Sahih International, unless otherwise stated. Other translations are referenced, for example, Hilali/Khan (last names of translators) and Pickthall.

[3] See question, 'Is Islam a religion of peace?' (pp. 93ff).

[4] See https://www.encounteringislam.org/muslim-world-facts

[5] Phrase coined by Dr Jay Smith of the Pfander Centre for Apologetics and PfanderFilms, USA.

[6] It is helpful to note that many Muslims are politically engaged and will often steer conversations toward political issues. Of course, this is not a bad thing. However, it can be unhelpful if you wish to move the conversation to more important questions – the pressing one being, "What do you think of Jesus?"

[7] The book of Hebrews is a wonderful explanation of the Old Testament's testimony to Jesus and the cross.

[8] LORD in the English translations of the Bible means Yahweh. Older English translations use Jehovah. It is the same name, said differently, depending on a person's dialect.

[9] There are many different titles given to God throughout the Scriptures, such as 'The Angel of the LORD' (Zechariah 3:6-7) and 'The Son of Man' (Daniel 7:13-14).

[10] There are numerous verses throughout the Bible, and here are a few to start with: Joshua 5:13-15; 1 Samuel 3:21; Job 19:23-27; Isaiah 7:14; John 1:14; Colossians 1:15; Hebrews 1:2-3; and Revelation 19:11-16.

[11] The so-called Gnostic Gospels were written far too late to be the authentic Gospels and were refuted by the Church leaders of the time.

[12] A read through the writings of the Church Fathers supports this claim. The Church Fathers discussed many in-house issues, and met to write public statements and confessions of faith in response to heretical teaching. Anyone who denied Jesus' divinity was considered a heretic. It was in response to the teachings of heretics, including the Gnostics, that many of the Church councils were called, and public statements made, reiterating what the Church had always believed. See 'Ante-Nicene Fathers, Nicene and Post-Nicene Fathers' edited by Philip Schaff. Also, see their writings here: https://www. ccel.org/fathers.html *Classics Ethereal Library: Bringing Christian classic books to life.*

[13] Whilst being careful not to over-stereotype, it can be helpful to keep in mind that some Western cultures have unspoken etiquette for conversations such as 'turn taking' and not talking over each other, while other cultures – more communal, extended family communities – proceed through conversations in a more 'free

for all' style. This can have an impact on how conversations progress if you are engaging with someone with different norms for conversation.

[14] Some Asian Islamic debaters such as Zakir Naik and Shabir Ally, specifically debating Christianity, have a large following worldwide and their arguments are often repeated in conversations with Christians.

[15] For a deeper study on who God is, consider downloading the course on the Trinity from https://www.onetruthproject.org/onlinecourses. The One Truth Project will continue to upload courses for those who are interested in delving deeper into key issues on theology, history, debunking myths, secularism, modern trends and Islam.

[16] Some Muslim friends will point to the Qur'anic verse which states, *"We have already created man... and We are closer to him than [his] jugular vein"*. However, because Allah is unknowable, and 'above us' according to Islamic theology (Q 50:16), most Muslims cannot explain what this verse means, as there is little Islamic theology to give it depth of meaning, or to make it a reality in the physical realm.

[17] Hilali and Khan translations use the expression "oh my slaves" [yāibādiya], the expression used in Arabic versions, while Sahih International and Yusuf Ali use "servants", which is not the sense of meaning found in the Arabic texts. The Qur'an does not teach a parent-child relationship between God and people. Rather, a master-slave relationship is far more apparent.

[18] Similar translation differences as in note 17 above.

[19] The Qur'an speaks of heavenly females waiting on men (Q 2:23-25; 3:14-15; 55:70-74; 72:55).

[20] Consider http://www.ecomena.org/food-wastes-ramadan/

[21] Note that we use the term 'Christian'. Some people sharing their faith with Muslims do not use this term. Yet we believe it makes things clearer when we call 'a spade a spade'. If your Muslim friend has misconceptions about Christianity, which is very likely, just clarify and explain. That is what we are called to do. *"But we have renounced the hidden things of shame, not walking in craftiness nor handling the word of God deceitfully, but by manifestation of the truth commending ourselves to every man's conscience in the sight of God"* (2 Corinthians 4:2). Some Christians like to use the term 'follower of Jesus'. There is nothing wrong with this, but it can muddy the waters. If a Muslim asks, "Are you a Christian?" Why not say, "Yes," especially as it identifies you with Christ. For clarification, you can follow this up with, "What do you think a Christian is?" If a Muslim knows you are a Christian, then they know who to come to when they have questions about the deeper issues of life, or about Christianity itself.

[22] *"O you who have believed, fight those adjacent to you of the disbelievers and let them find in you harshness. And know that Allah is with the righteous"* (Q 9:123).

[23] Note that the tomb of Muhammad has not been substantiated by any archaeological dig. This is true of most of Islam's traditional stories.

[24] See chart comparing Jesus and Muhammad (pp. 44,45).

[25] Ibn Ishaq, *The Life of Muhammad*, Alfred Guillaume (translator), Oxford University Press.

[26] Ibn Ishaq, *The Life of Muhammad*, pp. 68-69.

[27] In this chart we have abbreviated the Hadith references (Bukhari V1 bk1 h3); the full reference would be: Bukhari, Volume 1, Book 1, Hadith number 3. There are different referencing systems for Hadith. Printed references are often different from online references, although the Hadith number is more often consistent. Within charts, and where there are longer lists of Hadith, we usually reference the printed version unless otherwise stated. Until 2017, many researchers used the USC-MSA web (English) reference system, found online at sunnah.com or https://quranx.com/Hadiths. Due to extensive online referencing using the USC-MSA system, we have chosen to provide the USC-MSA reference alongside a hard copy reference from Darussalam publishers.

[28] Bukhari V7 bk76 h5686, p. 329 (Riyadh: Darussalam, 2015).

[29] Bukhari V7 bk76 h5686, p. 329; V2 bk24 h1501, p. 24 (Riyadh: Darussalam, 2015); Dawud V5 bk37 h4366-4367, p. 24 (Riyadh: Darussalam, 2008).

[30] Bukhari V5 bk63 h3929, p. 165 (Riyadh: Darussalam, 2015).

[31] The Qur'an is often ambiguous about whom it is addressing. Muslim scholars refer to the Tafsir (commentaries on the Qur'an) and Hadith (deeds and sayings of Muhammad) to try to understand what Qur'anic verses might mean. However, the task remains difficult, as there are contradictory explanations or contexts provided in the Islamic traditions.

[32] Bukhari V4 bk56 h3018, p. 56 (Riyadh: Darussalam, 2015).

[33] Dawud V5 bk37 h4353, h4366, h4370, pp. 24,26 (Riyadh: Darussalam, 2008).

[34] Bukhari V3 bk52 h2683, p. 496 (Riyadh: Darussalam, 2015); Bukhari V4 bk60 h3453-3454, p. 414 (Riyadh: Darussalam, 2015).

[35] Al-Tabari, *Volume 9: The Last Years of the Prophet*, Ismail Poonawala (translator) (State University of New York Press, p. 208). Al-Tabari is one of the primary sources of history (Tarikh) from an Islamic perspective.

[36] Only one such miraculous conception has ever been recorded.

[37] For a deeper understanding of God being with us in human form, creating and sustaining the world, see *Frameworks: Volume 1 - Roots* by Paul Blackham, pp. 23-37.

[38] The Sahih International translation uses the name "Jesus". However, this is not the correct translation. The Arabic word in the Qur'an is Īsā, yet this is not the name for Jesus in Arabic, which is Yasū, sometimes written as "Yassoua". It is this name which is found in the earliest Arabic translation of the Bible in 867 AD; https://www.arabicbible.com/codex-151.html. Scholars do not know where the name Isa comes from.

[39] For more comparisons between Jesus, Isa, and Muhammad see: https://www.onetruthproject.org/resources

[40] Hishām, A.M.I., et al. (1967), *The Life of Muhammad: A Translation of Ishāq's Sīrat Rasūl Allāh*, Oxford: Oxford University Press, pp. 106-107

[41] Translator Michael Fishbein, Al-Tabari, *The History of Al-Tabari: The Victory of Islam*, Vol. VII (Albany: New York Press, 1997), p. 3

[42] Bukhari V5, bk59, h462 (USC-MSA), Bukhari V5 bk 64 h4141 (Darussalam)

[43] Bukhari V6, bk61, h564 (USC-MSA), Bukhari V6 bk66 h5044 (Darussalam)

[44] Bukhari V4, bk54, h490 (USC-MSA), Bukhari V4 bk59 h3268 (Darussalam)

[45] For a more in-depth treatment of this see: http://www.answering-islam.org/Responses/Azmy/mhd_miracles.htm

[46] The life of Muhammad is not found in the Qur'an. It is found in the Sira (biography). Similarly, the context of Qur'anic verses are found in texts written much later, sometimes hundreds of years after the verses were written down. Details of Qur'anic contexts are found in the Tafsir (commentaries) and Tarikh (histories).

[47] It might be helpful to read these verses through with Muslim friends because it challenges disbelief in Jesus.

[48] See chart comparing Jesus and Muhammad (pp 44-45), and comparative, downloadable infographics at www.onetruthproject.org/resources. (Please note that they may be moved to a different place on the site over time).

[49] Note that some Muslims may try to argue that Jesus was a slave of Allah (Q 19:30) as a way to emphasise His humanity, and remove any reference to His divinity, but this comes from imposing the character of Isa onto Jesus.

[50] You may need to add that Jesus being a Prophet does not disqualify Him from also being Saviour (Matthew 1:21; 2 Timothy 1:10); King (John 18:36; Revelation 1:5) and Lord of us all (2 Corinthians 4:5; Philippians 2:11).

[51] Be aware that words in brackets in the English translations of the Qur'an are not usually in the Arabic texts. Qur'anic translators will add words for clarity (as in this example), or at times impose eisegesis (added meaning) from Islamic scholars on to the Qur'an, in order to better understand it. What is more, modern translations use the word Jesus instead of Isa. Yet, from a Biblical perspective the Isa of the Qur'an cannot be Jesus.

[52] English translations of the Qur'an insert the name Jesus into the Qur'anic text where the Arabic uses 'Isa'.

[53] Allah's Messenger said, "How will you be when the son of Maryam (Mary) [Isa] descends amongst you, and he will judge people by the law of the Qur'an and not by the law of the Gospel?" (Bukhari V4 bk 60 h3449, Darussalam)

[54] Bukhari V3 bk34 h2222, Darussalam

[55] We too should protest against the corruption of false teachers who rob the poor of their money to try appease the god they proclaim. There is a vast difference

between 'being a generous giver' like the Lord God, and taking money to appease a false god.

[56] Ed. Rizwi Faizer, *The Life of Muhammad: Al-Wāqidī* (New York: Routledge, 2011), pp. 85-86.

[57] The number can vary slightly depending on which Islamic source you read.

[58] Ibn Ishaq, *The Life of Muhammad*, Alfred Guillaume (translator), Oxford University Press, p. 464. See also: Al-Tabari, *Volume 8: Victory of Islam*, Michael Fishbein (translator), pp. 35-36.

[59] See *List of Killings Ordered or Supported by Muhammad* with references at: https://wikiislam.net/wiki/List_of_Killings_Ordered_or_Supported_by_Muhammad

[60] USC-MSA (https://quranx.com/Hadith/Muslim/USC-MSA/Book-10/Hadith-3901) or, English Translation of *Sahih Muslim*, Volume 4 (Riyadh: Darussalam, 2007), pp. 328-329.

[61] https://quranx.com/Hadith/Muslim/Reference/Hadith-1602

[62] Some of them are detailed here: http://www.answering-islam.org/BehindVeil/btv5.html

[63] Fernández-Morera, *Myth of the Andalusian Paradise*

[64] Azumah, J.A. (2014), *The Legacy of Arab-Islam in Africa: A Quest for Inter-Religious Dialogue* (Oneworld Publications); Davis, Robert C. (2003), *Christian Slaves, Muslim Masters: White Slavery in the Mediterranean, the Barbary Coast and Italy, 1500-1800* (Palgrave Macmillan). Also keep a look out for insights from Sarah Foster, *Colourism, Slavery and Islam*, DCCI Ministries, https://www.youtube.com/ watch?v=Bbo9nRcgkxY and hear Sarah discuss the *Treatment of Black Slaves* on The Jay Show from minute 6: https://www.youtube.com/watch?v=2WceXGdviFY

[65] "Those who follow the messenger, the Prophet who can neither read nor write, who they will find described in the Torah and the Gospel" (Q7:157 – Pickthall). (See: https://quranx.com/7.157 – Pickthall's translation is very clear on the traditional belief that Muhammad couldn't read or write).

[66] Just because Muslims claim Muhammad was from the line of Ishmael, and then by default, Abraham, that does not mean he really was. It is just a claim - a claim with no evidence to back it. That said, even if Muhammad did descend from Abraham, to truly belong to Abraham means to love and trust Abraham's LORD – the one who ate with him at the tents of Mamre in Genesis 18: "The LORD appeared to Abraham…"

[67] For more discussion of these texts see: http://www.answering-islam.org/Gilchrist/ muhammad.html

[68] Adapted from Power, B. (2015). "*Understanding Jesus and Muhammad: What the Ancient Texts Say about Them* (Acorn Press, Limited, p. 6). Note that we do not affirm the use of the word "Allah" as the personal name of God, although we recognise it might be used in recent Arabic non-Islamic books to refer to general references to god.

[69] See the One Truth Project website for a comparison between Jesus and Isa: www.onetruthproject.org/resources.

[70] *The Life of Muhammad*, Oxford: Oxford University Press, pp. 106-107

[71] *The Life of Muhammad*, Oxford: Oxford University Press, pp. 106-107

[72] For example, "When a person who has reached puberty and is sane, voluntarily apostatises from Islam, he deserves to be killed ..." Ed. Nuh Ha Mim Keller, *Reliance of the Traveller* (Maryland: Amana Publications, 1994) pp. 595-596

[73] Sahih al-Bukhari, 5:59:369; 1:3:106

[74] http://www.independent.co.uk/news/world/asia/christian-man-charged-with-blasphemy-in-pakistan-for-insulting-muhammad-in-whatsapp-poem-a7132231.html

[75] See http://corpus.quran.com/translation.jsp?chapter=33&verse=57 to read different versions.

[76] The greatest sin in Islam is called *shirk* (equating someone/something with Allah).

[77] Some will point to the concubines of Old Testament prophets – such as Hagar to Abraham. The use of a concubine is not an edict from God as His provision or way. Biblical accounts show that long-lasting domestic harm and pain result when we go against the way of the Lord. The story of Sarah and Hagar is one such example (Genesis 21).

[78] To compare different translations see: http://corpus.quran.com/translation.jsp?chapter=33&verse=50.

[79] Bukhari, 1:5:268; 7:62:142 (Darussalam).

[80] Al Tabari, *Volume 9: The Last Years of the Prophet*, Ismail K. Poonawala (translator), State University of New York Press, pp. 126-127.

[81] Bukhari, 5:58:234; 5:58:236; 7:62:64; 7:62:65; 7:62:88 (Darussalam). The last few references say that Aisha stayed with Muhammad for 9 years, until he died. The traditions say Muhammad was 63 (give or take a few years) when he died; see Sahih Bukhari, 5:58:190; 5:58:242; 5:58:243 (Darussalam).

[82] Be aware that Muslims today are trying to reinterpret their history by saying Aisha was much older. There is no support for this in any of the earliest texts of Islam. Furthermore, Q 65:4 has fuelled a debate among Muslims about whether pre-pubescent girls could be married and divorced.

[83] Al Tabari, *Volume 8: The Victory of Islam*, Michael Fishbein (translator), State University of New York Press, pp. 2-4; Al Tabari, *Volume 39: Biographies of the Prophet's Companions and Their Successors*, Ella Landau-Tasseron (translator), State University of New York Press, pp. 180-81; Tafsir al-Jalalayn on Sura 33:36-37; Tafsir al-Miqbas min Tafsir Ibn Abbas on Sura 33:36-37. For these quotations and more detail on this question see: http://www.answering-islam.org/Shamoun/zaynab.htm

[84] Muslims would not use personal pronouns to refer to Allah, since nothing in creation should be used to describe Allah in traditional Islamic belief. Christians, on the other hand, are free to use personal pronouns to speak of God because

God is a living Being, and has always walked with and communicated with us in ordinary human language. We are created in His image, male and female (Genesis 1:27-28).

[85] Some try to reinterpret this passage to be more favourable towards Islam. Yet, this is a modern manipulation of the text, and contrary to the instruction we are given – to read God's word with integrity (2 Corinthians 4:2-3).

[86] A Bible study on the book of Hebrews challenges much of what the Qur'an teaches about who God is, life, humans, sin, salvation and eternity. It reads like a commentary on the Old Testament.

[87] Ibn Ishaq, *The Life of Muhammad*, Alfred Guillaume (translator), Oxford University Press, p. 464. See also: Al Tabari, *Volume 8: Victory of Islam*, Michael Fishbein (translator), pp. 35-36.

[88] Or, Sunan Abu Dawud, Volume 5, Book 37, Hadith 4404 (Riyadh: Darussalam, 2008), p. 45.

[89] For further discussion and references on this incident see:
http://www.answering-islam. org/Authors/Arlandson/qurayza_jews.htm

[90] Ed. Rizwi Faizer, *The Life of Muhammad, al-Waqidi's Kitab al Maghazi* (New York: Routledge, 2011), pp. 383-384.

[91] Read the history of Muhammad according to Al Tabari referenced in the resources section.

[92] This can be clearly seen in the Islamic law manuals (Al-Quduri, Hanafi School of Law, p 661; Hanbali pp. 770-771) and the view of non-Muslims (Q 3:151, 8:12).

[93] See also Q 12:8, 9:5, 9:29, 47:4.

[94] There is no evidence of Arabic in the ancient archaeological record prior to the 4th century AD and even then it was Nabataean in makeup. Classical Arabic, which the Qur'an uses, was first introduced in the 6th century AD, and the earliest Qur'anic manuscripts use a Nabataean Aramaic form, which is derived from the area of Petra. See Pfanderfilms on YouTube for more details on the origins of Islam and the Qur'an.

[95] Jesus refers to God's name as His own. See Exodus 3:6,14,15,17; John 8:24, 28, 58.

[96] Before asking these questions, do read through them and consider answers that cohere with Biblical accounts.

[97] Even if you are unable to answer a question immediately, there are great resources (some included in this book) to find out how God would respond.

[98] According to Islamic tradition, Muhammad died in 632AD.

[99] The Dome's *Shahadah* states: *"la illaha illa-allah wahadu la sharikalah..."*, which translates as: "There is no god but God alone, He has no associates...". Islam denies the eternality and divinity of Christ and includes in its statement of faith a direct attack against the Byzantine Christian view of Jesus Christ.

[100] For the full text of the inscriptions on the Dome of the Rock see: http://www.islamicawareness.org/History/Islam/Inscriptions/DoTR.html

[101] Islam incorporates three stages of authority to judge how accurate a story in its traditions is: 1) Sahih = perfect 2) Hassan = not perfect 3) Da'if = weak

[102] A good critique of the Hadith is found in Bernie Power's book (2016): *Challenging Islamic Traditions: Searching Questions About the Hadith from a Christian Perspective* (Pasadena, California: William Carey Library Publishers).

[103] For example, Q 5:44-48; 5:65-68; 10:37; 32:23. For further discussion see: http://answering-islam.org/Campbell/s2c1.html

[104] See discussion on page 116 for a response to the allegation of the Bible having been corrupted.

[105] For details of these historians see: https://evidencetobelieve.net/history-of-jesus/

[106] Clement of Alexandria in *The Ante-Nicene Fathers: Vol 2, The Stromata/ Miscellanies* (New York: Cosimo, 2007), pp. 383-385; pp. 403-404.

[107] Tisdall, *The Original Sources of the Qur'an*, p. 133.

[108] Some writers, especially authors in the past, use 'Kuran/Koran'. In this book we have used 'Qur'an'.

[109] Guillaume, "The influence of Judaism on Islam", *The Legacy of Israel*, p. 134.

[110] See detail of citations at: http://www.biblestudymanuals.net/quran9e.htm

[111] Dr. Nelson Glueck, *Rivers in the Desert* (New York: Farrar, Straus and Cudahy, 1959), p.136. The One Truth Project runs Bible Tours in the British Museum, which show remarkable archaeological validation for the reliability of the Biblical accounts. Contact The One Truth Project at info@onetruthproject.org if you would like to join a tour.

[112] Dr. Jay Smith is in the process of producing many resources on this topic, in association with scholars from around the world. See his YouTube channel, *PfanderFilms,* at https://www.youtube.com/user/PfanderFilms.

[113] Founding Director General of IRCICA (1980-2004) and Secretary General of the Organisation of the Islamic Conference Research Centre

[114] Leading scholar in Qur'anic studies, ex-President of Turkish religious affairs, and a Deputy in the Turkish Parliament

[115] Dr. Tayyar Altıkulaç and Prof. Dr. Ekmeledin İhsanoğlu (Eds.), *Al-Mushaf a-Sharif, Attributed to 'Uthman bin 'Affān,* (Istanbul: IRCIC, 2007), pp. 10-35

[116] Altıkulaç, *Al-Mushaf al-Sharif*, 2007:41f

[117] Altıkulaç, *Al-Mushaf al-Sharif*, 2007:81

[118] Another "authoritative" Hadith (Sunni) is Mishkat al-Masabih, 14th century.

[119] This implies the permissibility of 'marital rape'.

[120] This verse supports the Islamic practice of Mutah (Muhammad's practice, followed today by Shi'ah Muslims) and Mysiar marriage (practiced by some

Sunni Muslims): Temporary – 3 hour or longer – 'marriages' for Muslim men who are away from their wives.

[121] Your Muslim friends might point you to women (in the West) not being able to vote until recent times. One way to counter this is to point to the many female queens in Christian-influenced nations, especially the Christian queens who carried great influence in the Middle Ages. The Podcast series, 'The First Steps of God' introduces this material at: @thefirststepsofGod on YouTube https://www.youtube.com/c/TheFirstStepsofGod

[122] Please note that the bracketed words are not in the Arabic text but are added in some translations, especially some intended for the West.

[123] See, for example, what Tafsir Ibn Kathir says on this verse: *"… 'those (slaves) whom your right hand possesses whom Allah has given to you', means, 'the slave-girls whom you took from the war booty are also permitted to you'. He owned Safiyyah and Juwayriyah, then he manumitted them and married them, and he owned Rayhana bint Sham'un AnNadariyyah and Mariyah Al-Qibtiyyah, the mother of his son Ibrahim, upon him be peace; they were both among the prisoners, may Allah be pleased with them."* http://www. qtafsir.com/index. php?option=com_content&task=view&id=1839&Itemid=89. Further discussion on this is available here: http://www.answeringmuslims.com/2014/02/does-islam-allow-muslims-to-rape-female.html.

[124] Most Arabic-speaking Christians use the word "*zawaj*" (pairing) instead of "*nikah*" for marriage. Islamic marriage is very different from Biblical marriage.

[125] There has never been any other understanding of what these verses mean through Islamic history. The references to 'What your right hands possess' in the Qur'an are objected to by some modern Islamic thinkers. If your Muslim friend objects to the traditional meaning, then ask what other possible meaning it could have, especially in the context of the verses in which it is found. Furthermore, the schools of Islamic law have instructions on how to gain, sell and treat slaves, including for sex. This is one of the reasons why we saw, and will continue to see, such extensive abuse of women captured by groups such as ISIS and Boko Haram. They are following the Islamic texts.

[126] Al Tabari V8, p. 117

[127] Guillaume/Ishaq, pp. 490-493; Al-Tabari, Vol. 9, p. 133; Al-Tabari, Vol. 39, pp. 182-184

[128] Guillaume/Ishaq, 653; Al-Tabari, Vol. 9, pp. 137,141; Al-Tabari, Vol. 39, pp. 193-195

[129] A list of 164 verses advocating violence is available here: http://www.answeringislam.org/Quran/Themes/jihad_passages.html

[130] Some Muslims may try to explain away the verses prescribing violence in Muhammad's last sermon (chapter 9) – one of the most authoritative chapters of the Qur'an, according to Islamic tradition. The traditions of Islam claim that the Jews broke a treaty, which is why upwards of 600 men were beheaded in one day, and their women and children taken as slaves. However, this argument

fails in the light of those very same traditions. It lists those who signed the treaty. The tribe that was beheaded was never part of the treaty – their names were not signatories to it, and only a handful of the tribe joined with the Meccans against Muhammad. Yet, even if they had been signatories, or if the whole tribe had decided against Muhammad, it still begs the question as to how the 'prophet' of Islam had any moral standing left after beheading hundreds and taking their women as sex slaves, simply for not submitting to his rule.

[131] See 'Question on Abrogation' (pp. 97ff)

[132] The point is that beliefs can only really be judged by God, not by humans. God will ultimately judge people for their unbelief. Human governments condemn people for evil actions (Romans 13) such as abuse and murder.

[133] At the end of the book, we will briefly respond to verses sceptics might point to regarding their misconceptions of "violence in the Bible"(pp 125ff).

[134] Trans. Nuh Ha Mim Keller, *Reliance of the Traveller* (Maryland: Amana Publications, 1994). It is attributed largely to al-Nawawi, a 13th century authoritative Shafi'i scholar. The volume is seen as "one of the finest and most reliable short works in Shafi'i jurisprudence" (p. vii). Pages 595-613 deal with apostasy from Islam; what is considered apostasy; Jihad; objectives of Jihad; rules of warfare; spoils of battle; and *al-dhimma* (non-Muslims living in and subject to an Islamic state).

[135] Shi'a and/or Liberal Muslims do not always accept the Sunni traditions about Muhammad's life and sayings. Also be aware that many Muslims pick and choose which Hadith they accept, and in conversation this often becomes apparent by their rejection of the many Hadith you might use. That said, in order to know the facts about Muhammad's life, Muslims need to move outside the Qur'an, to the biographies and the Hadith.

[136] Bukhari V8 Bk86 h6799 (Darussalam)

[137] Bukhari V8 bk85 h6773 (Darussalam)

[138] Bukhari V8 bk86 h6802-4 (Darussalam)

[139] These verses are taken from the Hilali/Khan translation of the Qur'an into English (Darussalam Publications); see Resources section for more details.

[140] The historical context of a Qur'anic verse is called '*asbaab al-nuzul*' in Arabic.

[141] Mark Durie, *Is Islam a Religion of Peace?*, Independent Journal Review (2015); https://www.meforum.org/5715/islam-religion-of-peace

[142] Mark Durie, *Is Islam a Religion of Peace?*, Independent Journal Review (2015); https://www.meforum.org/5715/islam-religion-of-peace

[143] Qur'an Tafsir Ibn Kathir 2:11 http://m.qtafsir.com/Surah-Al-Baqara/Meaning-of-Mischief

[144] For a more detailed treatment of this question see: https://christianconcern.com/ resource/is-islam-a-religion-of-peace/

[145] Trans. Tahir Mahmood Kiani, *The Mukhtasar, Al-Quduri, Al-Baghdadi (362-428AH [973-1037AD]): A Manual of Islamic Law according to the Hanafi School* (London: Ta-Ha Publishers, 2012²), pp. 661-662.

[146] Shaykh Salih ibn Fawzan al-Fawzan, *A Commentary on Zad al-Mustaqni': Imam al-Hajjawai's (d.968 [1561AD]) Classical Guide to the Hanbali Madhab* (Birmingham, UK: Dar al-Arqam Publishing, 2016), pp. 765-766.

[147] For more discussion on abrogation refer http://www.answering-islam.org/Authors/Farooq_Ibrahim/abrogation.htm. Also http://www.meforum.org/1754/peace-or-jihadabrogation-in-islam.

[148] Alfred Guillume, *The Life of Muhammad: A Translation of ibn Ishaq's Sirat Rasul Allah* (Karachi, Pakistan: Oxford University Press, 1982), pp. 71-73 and 104-107

[149] Bukhari, V6 bk61 h509-514 (USC-MSA), V6 bk 66 h4986 (Darussalam)

[150] News of Qur'anic folios found in Birmingham University were highlighted in the media as the "world's oldest Koran" although the folios constitute only 33 verses whereas the Qur'an has 6,236. (See 'World's oldest Koran: Birmingham reacts to the discovery': https://www.bbc.co.uk/news/uk-england-birmingham-33624954). Furthermore, the carbon dating of the sleeves of folios are troubling for Muslims because they are likely to have been written before Muhammad received his revelation! What's more, these stories are all pre-Islamic and existed hundreds of years before the Qur'an was even purported to have been written. They are pre-Qur'anic Arabic stories, borrowed much later, and incorporated into the Qur'an in the 8th century. The latest research tells us it took 150 years to compile/write a Qur'an that is similar to the ones Muslims use today, although still not the same.

[151] For a deeper insights into this topic see PfanderFilms' YouTube channel at https//www.youtube.com/user/PfanderFilms. Some Muslim friends might say these are polemical videos, and disregard them. However, the content is what is most important; they simply raise questions that anyone concerned about truth would want answers to.

[152] Called *"tanzil"* (Q 4:61)

[153] Islamic traditions are divided into two categories, 1) Mansukh, meaning former, or weak and 2) Nasikh, meaning later, or strong. Traditionally, the later, strong verses, abrogate the earlier, weak verses.

[154] Salman Rushdie, *The Satanic Verses*, Random House, 1988. For more background on the repercussions following the publication of this book see: https://christianconcern.com/resource/from-fatwa-to-fear-30-years-on-from-the-satanic-verses-affair/

[155] A detailed exposition of this issue is available here:
http://www.answering-islam.org/ Responses/Saifullah/sverses.htm

[156] These questions require that you have a good understanding of the verses and the arguments that you are presenting.

[157] For further discussion see http://www.answering-islam.org/authors/vargo/rebuttals/ibnanwar/crucifixion_egypt.html

[158] For an exciting tour of archeological discoveries that confirm the historical accuracy of Biblical records, join the One Truth Tour of the Bible in the library of the British Museum: https://www.onetruthproject.org/museum-tours or email info@onetruthproject.org for more information.

[159] For further discussion see here: http://www.answering-islam.org/Responses/Saifullah/ dirham.htm

[160] For further discussion see here: http://www.answering-islam.org/Quran/Contra/qbhc01.html

[161] For further discussion see here: http://www.answering-islam.org/Responses/Saifullah/ezra.htm

[162] For more information on Mary in Islam see http://www.message4muslims.org.uk/christ/the-incarnation-of-christ/mary-in-islam/

[163] For more on this topic see Dan Brubaker's work on the Qur'an: https://www.danielbrubaker.com/daniel-brubaker-quran-and-islam/

[164] Of the Topkapi and other early manuscripts, Dr. Ekmeleddin Ihsanoğlu in his study, *Al-Mushaf al-Sharif* (2007), claims, "... we have none of Uthman's Mushafs" (p. 10).

[165] Of the Sammarqand, Dr Tayyar Altıkulaç, co-researcher with Ihsanoğlu, also admits these Mushafs "are not Uthmanic", with 2,270 consonantal differences (p. 81). "... no discipline of spelling, different ways of writing the same word, scribal mistakes, copyists' mistakes ..." (pp. 71-72).

[166] Of the Al Husseini, Francois Deroche dates it to the 9th century; Altıkulaç admits this is not from Uthman.

[167] Of the Paris Petropolitanus, Francois Deroche points out "corrections". It "disagrees with the Cairene Mushaf in 93 places", claims that it is "later modified with erasures and additions" and that it includes only "26% of the Qur'an".

[168] Altıkulaç dates it to early 8th century; Lings dates it to late 8th century.

[169] For excellent research on this topic, visit PfanderFilms' YouTube channel, https://www.youtube. com/watch?v=lXzWzhVKXjM

[170] Visit PfanderFilms' YouTube channel at https://www.youtube.com/watch?v= HS3pCDksDkM&list=PL0TKiKX1srq2y3ETpJd8I5gUtUeBQ13m4&index=7.

[171] For further discussion on this point see: https://www.answering-islam.org/authors/shamoun/q_confirms_t1.html

[172] For further discussion refer to http://www.answering-islam.org/Responses/Shabir-Ally/q14_prophecy.htm

[173] To see this illustrated with a selection of passages, some of which are from the Qur'an and others from elsewhere, see http://answering-islam.org/Nehls/Ask/like.html

[174] Often, Muslims tend to have a magical view of the Qur'an. To many Muslims the words are not as important as the sound of text; in some parts of the Muslim world worshippers fall into a trance as the Qur'an is recited.

[175] Alfred J. Hoerth, *Archaeology and the Old Testament* (Grand Rapids: Baker Books, 1998). To join a tour of *The Bible in the British Museum*, contact the One Truth Project at info@onetruthproject.org or book a tour at: http://www.onetruthproject.org/museum-tours

[176] All these, and many of the questions addressed in this book, are covered in One Truth Project's online course. For more information contact One Truth Project at: info@onetruthproject.org

[177] For further discussion see https://www.answering-islam.org/Hahn/son.html

[178] Sceptics may argue that 'the Ancient of Days' is not the Father, and that 'the man with an everlasting Kingdom' whom all nations will worship, is not the Son. Who then are they, if this is not who they are? They aren't angels, nor are they human beings. Only God is worshipped by people from all nations, and obtains an everlasting kingdom. The 'Son of man' figure can be none other than a divine figure.

[179] For a deeper understanding refer to the very helpful Bible study, *Exodus,* in the Book by Book series by Dr Paul Blackham: http://biblicalframeworks.com

[180] For further discussion see http://www.answering-islam.org/Nehls/Answer/corrupt.html. For a detailed discussion of this question see: Nickel, Gordon D. (2015), *The Gentle Answer to the Muslim Accusation of Biblical Falsification.* Calgary: Bruton Gate Publishing.

[181] See question 'Did you know that the Qur'an testifies to the inspiration of the Bible?' (p 74).

[182] For a detailed critique of the Muslim accusation of Biblical corruption see, Nickel, Gordon D. (2015), *The Gentle Answer to the Muslim Accusation of Biblical Falsification.* Calgary: Bruton Gate Publishing.

[183] There is a tradition of the separation of church and state in Christianity. Adherents point to the way that the prophets challenged the kings and rulers in the Old Testament, and to Jesus' response, *"Render to Caesar the things that are Caesar's, and to God the things that are God's"* (Mark 12:17). This means that rulers are held to account. Islam, however, does not separate religion from political rule.

[184] Articles addressing trends in society can be found at https://christianconcern.com

[185] The First Steps of God podcast (Episodes 1-3) discusses 'freedom' in some depth: @thefirststepsofgod, on YouTube, Spotify, iTunes and Facebook. All the episodes may be found at https://www.onetruthproject.org/podcast.

[186] Dario Fernandez-Morera, *Myth of the Andalusian Paradise*, p. 129.

[187] Ed. Rizwi Faizer, *The Life of Muhammad: Al-Waqidi's Kitab al-Maghazi* (New York: Routledge, 2011).

[188] *The History of al-Tabari*, Volumes 8, 9, 10, 12, 13, 14 (State University of New York Press).

[189] Sebastien Mamerot (1472-1474), *A Chronicle of the Crusades*, Taschen-Bibliotheca Universalis. Another excellent resource is: Stark, Rodney (2010), *God's Battalions: The Case for the Crusades* (New York: Harper One).

[190] Jude 5 tells us specifically who the Lord is: "Jesus" (ESV translation). Be aware that some English versions do not mention Jesus in this passage.

[191] Biblical prayer (formal and individual) is communion with the Lord. Islamic formal prayer (salat) is an act of obedience – a set deed which must be done.

[192] Human beings often reduce God to a static simplistic being, incapable of relationship, as if God is a singular entity, unconnected to us and His creation in any way. However, to call God 'Father', 'Son' and 'Holy Spirit means that God, although in many ways wholly unlike us, is also very like us – indescribable, and yet describable, unseen yet seen.

[193] For an excellent in-depth, but easy to read, theological series on God see: *Frameworks Volume 1. Roots: 30 Days of Theology and Bible Study*, (Biblical Frameworks: 2019), by Dr. Paul Blackham.

[194] The NIV reads: "... he persevered because he saw him who is invisible" (Hebrews 11:27).

[195] Some of your Muslim friends may disregard these websites as 'polemical' and not valid, simply because they ask tough questions of Islam. Even if you do not wish to refer your friends to these websites, their content including the questions they pose, are nevertheless legitimate. It is worth noting that most Islamic websites which deal with Christian material are polemical against Christianity, but that does not mean we should ignore the questions that Muslims ask.

Recommended Resources

Further teaching on these questions and in-depth responses:

Websites
Christian Concern regularly posts articles about Islam and its increasing influence.
https://christianconcern.com/ccissues/islam/

One Truth Project develops resources and runs courses on Islam:
https://www.onetruthproject.org

Answering Islam has articles about various questions Muslims ask: *http://www.answering-islam.org/*

Answering Muslims has articles about Islam by David Wood:
http://www.answeringmuslims.com/ [195]

PfanderFilms has videos on the historical critique of Islam:
https://www.youtube.com/channel/UC-wOxG8p_Nk5nFkSxZOxq6w

Social Media
@CConcern

@OneTruthProject

@TheFirstStepsofGod

Source Material

Qur'an
Various translations of the Qur'an are available at www.quran.com or corpus.quran.com

Hadith
Khan, Muhammad Muhsin (Translator) Sahih al-Bukhari, Volumes 1, 3, 4, 5, 6, 7 (Riyadh: Darussalam)

The Hadith are available at:
https://sunnah.com/ or *http://quranx.com/Hadiths*

However, the Hadith online are not always easy to find, and references can change, depending on what system is used. For this book we have used the Arabic/English Hadith series published by Darussalam, Riyadh and then double-checked the content with other online platforms.

Sirah
Guillume, Alfred, *The Life of Muhammad: A Translation of Ibn Ishaq's Sirat Rasul Allah* (Karachi: Oxford University Press, 1982). This is considered a classic on the life of Muhammad.

Islamic Law
Keller, Nuh Ha Mim, *Reliance of the Traveller* (Maryland: Amana Publications, 1994). This is a classic manual of Islamic law. It is attributed largely to al-Nawawi, a 13th century authoritative Shafi'i scholar. The volume is seen as *'one of the finest and most reliable short works in Shafi'i jurisprudence'* (p vii).

Kiani, Tahir Mahmood (translator), *The Mukhtasar, Al-Quduri, Al-Baghdadi (362-428AH [973-1037AD]) – A Manual of Islamic Law according to the Hanafi School* (London: Ta-Ha Publishers, 2010).

Shaykh Salih ibn Fawzan al-Fawzan, *A Commentary on Zad al-Mustaqni': Imam al-Hajjawai's (d.968 [1561AD]) Classical Guide to the Hanbali Madhab* (Birmingham, UK: Dar al-Arqam Publishing, 2016).

Islamic History
Al Tabari is a primary source for traditional Islamic history. The volumes are available in PDF form online with URLs similar to this: https://kalamullah.com/Books/The%20History%20Of%20Tabari/ Tabari_Volume_01.pdf

Al Tabari, Volume 8, *The Victory of Islam*, Michael Fishbein (translator), (State University of New York Press).

Al Tabari, Volume 9, *The Last Years of the Prophet*, Ismail K. Poonawala (translator), (State University of New York Press, 1990).

Al-Tabari, Volume 10, *The Conquest of Arabia*, Fred M Donner (translator), (State University of New York Press, 1993).

Al-Tabari, Volume 11, *The Challenge to the Empires*, Yahya Blankinship (translator), (State University of New York Press, 1993).

Al-Tabari, Volume 12, *The Battle of al-Qadisiyyah and the Conquest of Syria and Palestine*, Yohanan Friedman (translator), (State University of New York Press, 1992).

Al-Tabari, Volume 12, *The Conquest of Iraq, Southwestern Persia and Egypt*, Gautier H. A. Juynboll (translator), (State University of New York Press, 1989).

Al Tabari, Volume 14, *The Conquest of Iran*, G. Rex Smith (translator), (State University of New York Press, 1994).

Al Tabari, Volume 39, *Biographies of the Prophet's Companions and Their Successors*, Ella Landau-Tasseron (translator), (State University of New York Press, 1998).

Further Helpful Titles
Particularly recommended books are indicated with an annotation.

Allen, Stafford (2016), *My Muslim Neighbour: Communicating well with your Muslim friend* (Gilead Books) – A very helpful resource on discussing faith with Muslims.

Blackham, Paul (2007), *Exodus: Book by Book: The Joy of Meeting Jesus in All the Scriptures* (London: Biblical Frameworks) – An excellent book and Bible study explaining the Gospel from the books of Moses.

Brubaker, Daniel Alan (2019), *Corrections in Early Qur'an Manuscripts: Twenty Examples* (Lovettsville: Think and Tell Press).

Coxe, Arthur Cleveland and Donaldson, Sir James and Roberts, Rev Alexander (eds) (2007), *The Ante-Nicene Fathers: Volume II* (New York: Cosimo books).

Davis, Robert C. (2003), *Christian Slaves, Muslim Masters: White Slavery in the Mediterranean, the Barbary Coast and Italy, 1500-1800* (London: Palgrave Macmillan).

Durie, Mark (2010), *The Third Choice: Islam, Dhimmitude and Freedom* (Melbourne: Deror Books) – very good on Dhimmitude, i.e. the status of non-Muslims under Islamic rule.

Durie, Mark (2014), *Which God? Jesus, Holy Spirit, God in Christianity and Islam* (Melbourne: Deror Books)

Faizer, Ed. Rizwi (2011), *The Life of Muhammad: Al-Waqidi's Kitab alMaghazi* (New York: Routledge) – called 'the raids', a detailed early biography describing Muhammad's life as a prophet.

Geisler, Norman L., and Abdul Saleeb (1993), *Answering Islam* (Michigan: Baker Books) – a great overview of Islamic apologetics.

Holland, Tom (2012), *In the Shadow of the Sword: The Battle for Global Empire and the End of the Ancient World* (London: Abacus) – a popular book that raises important questions about the origins of Islam.

Hoerth, Alfred J. (1998), *Archaeology and the Old Testament* (Grand Rapids: Baker Books).

İhsanoğlu, Ekmeledin & Altıkulaç, Tayyar (ed.) (2007), *Al-Mushaf al-Sharif* – an investigation by two Muslim academics into the manuscript of one of the six earliest Qur'ans in existence today [currently out of print but available in some academic libraries].

McDowell, Josh, (1999), *New Evidence Demands a Verdict* (Nashville: Thomas Nelson Publishers).

Morera, Dario Fernandez (2016), *The Myth of the Andalusian Paradise: Muslims, Christians, and Jews under Islamic Rule in Medieval Spain* (Open Road Media) – a well-researched and documented book on what really happened when Islam invaded Europe in the middle ages.

Maurer, Andreas (2011), *Ask Your Muslim Friend* (Xulon Press) – a helpful book on what Muslims believe, and questions you could ask them.

Nickel, Gordon D. (2015), *The Gentle Answer to the Muslim Accusation of Biblical Falsification* (Calgary: Bruton Gate) – a very thorough response to the Muslim accusation of corruption against the Bible.

Power, Bernie (2015), *Understanding Jesus and Muhammad: What the Ancient Texts Say about Them* (Bible Society Australia) – excellent resource comparing Jesus and Muhammad according to the Bible and the Qur'an.

Power, Bernie (2016), *Challenging Islamic Traditions: Searching Questions about the Hadith from a Christian Perspective* (William Carey Library) – very helpful resource on the Hadith.

Qureshi, Nabeel (2014), *Seeking Allah, Finding Jesus: A Devout Muslim Encounters Christianity* (Grand Rapids, Michigan: Zondervan) – an insightful book of a Muslim man's journey from Islam to Christ; recommended to give to Muslim friends.

Qureshi, Nabeel (2016), *No God but One: Allah or Jesus? A Former Muslim Investigates the Evidence for Islam and Christianity* (Zondervan) – a useful introduction to apologetics tackling Islam. Qureshi, N. (2016), *Answering Jihad: A Better Way Forward* (Zondervan) – excellent short summary of the teaching of Jihad in Islam.

Rushdie, Salman (1988), *The Satanic Verses,* (Random House).

Shah, Hannah (2009), *The Imam's Daughter* (London: Rider) – a gripping autobiographical story. Highly recommended.

Sheikh, Bilquis and Richard Schneider (1979), *I Dared to Call Him Father* (Kingsway) – superb testimony of a conversion from Islam and recommended for giving to Muslims.

Shumack, Richard (2011), *Witnessing to Western Muslims*, vol. 9 (Latimer Briefing; London: The Latimer Trust) – a useful book on the subject.

Solomon, Sam and Atif Debs (2016), *Not the Same God: Is the Qur'anic Allah the Lord God of the Bible?* (London: Wilberforce Publications) – a detailed rebuttal of the claim that Christians and Muslims worship the same God.

Spencer, Robert (2006), *The Truth About Muhammad* (Washington: Regency Publishing) – a look at the life of Muhammad, from Islamic sources.

Spencer, Robert (2007), *Religion of Peace? Why Christianity Is and Islam Isn't* (Washington: Regency Publishing) – a helpful comparison of Christianity and Islam.

Spencer, Robert (2012), *Did Muhammad Exist? An Inquiry into Islam's Obscure Origins* (Wilmington, Delaware: ISI Books) – fascinating insight into the lack of historical corroboration for the traditional stories around Muhammad and the founding of Islam. Check for revised editions.

Stark, Rodney (2010), *God's Battalions: The Case for the Crusades* (New York: Harper One) – an excellent resource on the crusades.

Strobel, Lee (1998), *The Case for Christ*, (Zondervan).

Tisdal, W. St. Clair (2014), *The Original Sources of the Qur'an: Its Origin in Pagan Legends and Mythology* (Alev Books, from 1905).

Warraq, Ibn (2003), *Why I Am Not a Muslim* (New York: Prometheus) – a detailed critique of Islam by a former Muslim, who is now an atheist.

White, James R. (2013), *What Every Christian Needs to Know About the Qur'an* (Minneapolis: Bethany House Publishers) – very helpful material on the Qur'an.

Ye'or, Bat (2005), *The Dhimmi: Jews and Christians under Islam* (Fairleigh Dickinson University Press).

Some Helpful Online Resources
Podcast: *The First Steps of God, www.onetruthproject.org/podcast* – short podcasts responding to myths and legends circulating in secular and Muslim societies

OneTruth online course: *www.onetruthproject.org/onlinecourses*

www.onetruthproject.org/current-issues – short articles on world events concerning Islam.

biblicalframeworks.com – excellent Bible discussion on Jesus throughout the Scriptures, particularly in the Old Testament.

The Bible in the British Museum: *www.onetruthproject.org/museum-tours* – a two-hour tour looking at archaeological discoveries which confirm the historical accuracy and reliability of the Biblical record.

Articles from Christian Concern:
Is Islam a Religion of Peace?
https://christianconcern.com/resource/is-islam-a-religion-of-peace/

What is Islamophobia?
https://christianconcern.com/comment/what-is-islamophobia/

The Challenge of Islam in the UK
https://christianconcern.com/resource/the-challenge-of-islam-in-the-uk/

Printed in Great Britain
by Amazon

13530066R00086